SEVEN CENTURIES OF THE PROBLEM
OF CHURCH AND STATE

SEVEN CENTURIES
OF THE PROBLEM OF
CHURCH AND STATE

❦

FRANK GAVIN

NEW YORK

Howard Fertig

1971

To

HUGHELL EDGAR WOODALL FOSBROKE

FOREWORD

THE honor done me in inviting me to deliver the Spencer Trask Lectures March 29-April 1, 1937, impels me to express my great sense of gratitude and deep appreciation for the opportunity afforded me. The hospitality of colleagues at Princeton, the visits with old and the making of new friends, and the graciousness of the group before whom the lectures were delivered combined to make of the occasion one to which I shall always look back with the warmest gratification. Especially I beg to thank those whose hospitality was so generously extended to me and particularly express my sense of indebtedness to Professor Hoyt Hudson and the Reverend John S. Crocker, who was so good as to read a portion of my fourth lecture. My great thanks are due to the Librarian of the Theological Seminary for his unfailing kindness and assistance, which were put to a severe test in the demands I made upon him. Finally, I beg to express my indebtedness to the careful and competent work of Miss Katharine C. Jones, which has made possible not only the preparation of the text but its revision and final form.

CONTENTS

I

INTRODUCTION

IN the whole problem of the relations between Church and State there are two fundamental poles: First and foremost is the theological issue, and depending upon what you think the Church is will be the Church's attitude toward the State; the other pole is the practical and historical exigency, and again and again in human history men have had to make compromises, sacrificing principle in order to provide opportunity for the necessary minimum fulfilment of so much as can be salvaged from a situation theoretically impossible. As an illustration of the former, one can point to the Lutheran attitude, that of the state-created Evangeliche Kirche in Germany since 1817, and the Calvinistic theocratic State wherever it has existed without let or hindrance. As illustration of the latter, one can name the not too well known status of Christian opinion in the early Roman Empire under the pagan emperors, and the present-day condition of the patriarchal Church of Moscow with relation to the Soviet régime. It would seem to me that the fundamental issue as between Church and State revolves about one of these two axes. In other words, it is the old matter of theory and practice, of adjustment of principle to actuality, of divergent convictions and adjustment to reality. Seldom, however, in history have these been brought out in pure color, for conflicting interests inevitably have arisen, since both personalities and accidents have played their part in given historical situations. Granted these facts, let us consider rather more closely some of the theological issues involved.

The "Church" may be considered to be a divine institution, supernaturally founded, endowed by God and governed by the Holy Spirit, the compass of whose domain extends over the whole of the human life from the cradle through the grave to the Here-after. It is obvious that if one so believes in the Church, a compromise in theory with any type of totalitarian State is entirely excluded. The Gregorian theory of the Middle Ages and the theological con-victions of a St. Ignatius Loyola, while different from each other, still agree in this that there can be only one fundamental loyalty for the Christian, and that is to his Church. The omnicompetent Church in con-flict with a totalitarian State is at least in principle bound to produce a battle to the death. As we shall see when we consider the doctrine of Hildebrand, there is no room for the admission of any sacredness of title to the sovereignty of the State; all that the State has derives from the approval by the Church of its claims. So long, therefore, as the State is sub-servient and docile, governed and directed by the Church, it has a right to man's allegiance and his obedience; so far as there is concerned a parity of powers the Hildebrandian theory is entirely negative in its attitude. There can be no such parity. The tra-dition of Hildebrand, later Gregory VII, has been carried on not only through the Middle Ages but into modern times by the Society of Jesus. It takes a very slight acquaintance with the *Ratio Studiorum* or the "Spiritual Exercises" to convince the reader that they are of the same spirit as the great Hildebrand's. Perhaps this is the most complete example of the omnicompetent Church claiming to govern and control the civil State, directing its ideals, and with regard to it holding as its chief principle the fact that the supernatural man supersedes the natural man, and that the latter is not only born in sin but continues so to be until such time as in every respect he submits himself to the Church. As in the individual case so in that of organized society: the State must be baptized, disciplined, directed, and formed and enslaved by the supernatural society of the Church.

An alternative theory would be to put the sacredness of the secular on a parity with the supernatural institution, the Church. Of necessity it would have to disclaim many of the alleged sanctions for the institution called the Church as existing in time and space in history. Such matters as polity—for example—whether there be any divinely instituted ministry, any definitive organization which must of necessity hold sway, and not only claim but demand as a right, man's allegiance thereto—would be as much out of the picture as the matter of divine sanction for creedal statements, standards of worship and other like essential matters. If the Church be considered to be a *congregatio predestinatorum*, the exact membership of which is known only to God, then the visible society of Christians here on earth possesses no authority whatever derived from God of any mandatory quality or of any single sanction. Possibly at the extreme pole (so far as concerns a doctrine of the Church) from that of the Gregorian ideal would stand the theory of the free churches and the Lutheran

Church. The latter group has been secure and certain that the State is ordained of God, but believes that the Church on earth as a visible, corporate society is rather a training school for Christianity than the authoritative body possessing a mandate from the Almighty. That this set of ideas was not lacking in the Middle Ages may be apparent from what follows in the succeeding pages. The enormous support and vast importance of such a theory, for example, as that neither baptism nor ordination convey grace but are, as rites, the public recognition of the bestowal of grace already given individually by direct action of the Holy Spirit, is closely bound up with a whole theory of Church and State and a theory of sovereignty. For the problem of sovereignty is the real axis about which the whole controversy arises: To which power does man owe primary allegiance—to the ecclesiastical institution, or the civil? In other words, it is the matter of what for lack of better terms we have to define as Church and State.

It is a commonplace of history that the institutions which man has found most valuable and essential to his welfare sooner or later are invested with Divine sanction. Whenever in the process of human experience either institution, whether Church or State, becomes discredited, the almost inevitable tendency would be enormously to invest with divine sanctions that institution which at the time would seem of the greater value. The evils, for example, of the fourteenth century brought about a large-scale discrediting of clericalism and of disillusionment with the hierarchic organization. With reference to the established ecclesiastical hierarchy, the tradition emanating from

Machiavelli in his *Il Principe* would seem to have a direct bearing upon the creation of the modern secularist State. It in turn had its earlier antecedents in the Middle Ages and in part formulated what certain groups of men were thinking and in part took a new stand in directing thought.

Again, much of the controversy between the claims of the Church and the claims of the State will, I hope, appear in the pages that follow, to be, so far as the anti-papal writers are concerned, an attempt to re-deem and rejustify the divine authority of the State. The theory of the divine right of kings had a reputable ancestry. It had the merit of binding together both the classical Greek tradition as embodied in Roman law, and certain elements of the Christian tradition, which together made self-respecting the doctrine of the State as over against one stream of thinking deriving from St. Augustine, and going through some of the Latin Fathers to Gregory VII.

In society, organized as it was in classical times as well as in the Middle Ages, sheer individualism was unthinkable. Authority, law, the conception of justice, of obligation, of duty, were fundamental in the processes of all men's thinking. Whenever this secular order was in grave danger of being entirely swamped by the ecclesiastical, whenever the hierarchy would either in theory or practice seem to have it all their way, a certain demoralization and degradation of the mind must inevitably have set in on the part of the ruler and the secular authority. So it would seem to be not only a matter of principle but also an exigency of concrete situations in history which periodically produced bursts of anti-curialism and reassertions of the doctrine of the divine right of kings.

The Protestant Reformation was never more medieval than in its assertion of this principle of divine authority having been given to the ruler. It could be best stated in the three phases of the divine right of kings developed during and after the English Reformation. My reading of history convinces me that what is called the "Reformation" in England was a process of over a century's duration. Under the Tudors, the divine right of kings was a constitutional program; under the Stuarts it became also a matter of dogma and doctrine; with the rise of the Non-Jurors we reach a stage which can hardly be called anything but sentimental. Even a cursory acquaintance with the documents of the English Reformation would show how strongly this ancient and medieval doctrine played an impelling rôle in the issues of English history whether of the Church or of the State.[1] Henry VIII went back to Justinian for his plan and program. Elizabeth utilized not only the constitutional principle but began the process of dogmatizing the doctrine of the divine right of kings. In the little known Canons of 1606, commonly called Bishop Overall's Convocation Book,[2] the Church of England put itself on record unanimously in the convocations of both provinces as asserting this political theory to be binding in conscience as deriving from divine revelation. It is somewhat ironic to discover that what made these canons inoperative as permanent and normative documents of Anglican Church history was the fact that the royal assent was withheld. The King who believed in his own divine right, actually prevailed upon the Church to withhold probably the quaintest and most extraordinary statement of that doctrine.[3]

JUSTINIAN

To understand the ideal which Justinian had before him, with special reference to Church and State, it is necessary to go back to some of the hidden assumptions and premises not only of his thinking but of the whole mass of legislative statements that had preceded him. Between the years 529-534 he brought out the Justinianic Code, which was an extensive revision of the previous Theodosian Code, badly needed because of the increasing complexity and confusion of the material, together with the new ideas which would necessarily entail as well a criticism as a revision of the inherited tradition. Needless to say, the tradition was both of the old Roman pagan law and also constituted of the Christian interpretation thereof. About 533 he gave over to Tribonian the task of editing the *Pandects*. A third series of legislative documents, comprising the actual work of his own lifetime, was published after his death under the title *Novellae*.

Few students in the West have done justice to the enormous importance of Justinian's work. Many know of him as the man who recovered most of the domains of Constantine and reconstituted the Roman Empire. Everyone knows of the building, under his direction, of the greatest church in Christendom, Sancta Sophia (532-537). But as the most conspicuous theologian of the sixth century and the formulator of the ideal which to this day flourishes as normative for the whole of Eastern Christendom, and

constitutes the obverse of that of which Sovietism is
the reverse and to an overwhelming extent conditioned the English Reformation and the consequent
history of Anglicanism, there is little general knowledge of Justinian.

At the outset it may be well then for us to consider
in very rapid survey what Justinian had to deal with
by way of inherited material for his own convictions,
in regard to the question of Church and State. I shall
speak briefly first of the New Testament and its tradition, together with the background which underlay
it; then pass on to a comment or two with regard to
Patristic material; and finally invite your attention
to a consideration of some of the things which come
into clear light in the fourth century.

When the Lord Christ said[4] "Therefore render unto
Caesar the things that are Caesar's and to God the
things that are God's," what did He mean? It would
seem at first sight certain that He inculcates the principle that the believing Christian would be a citizen
of two worlds at the same time, with a double obligation—to God, and to the head of the State.[5] The early
Church construed the passage to signify that there
were two claims on the believer, the adjustment of
which was an essential part of his Christian life. If,
on the other hand—as the Apocalyptic school insists
—this passage belongs to those statements of Christ
which have to do only with a temporary reference,
His words would mean: "Inasmuch as the present
condition of affairs will soon pass away, the first as
well as the simplest thing to do is to conform to the
actualities of the case for the time being only, since
the eternal is about to burgeon into time and the

whole of the present fashion of things will be dis-
sipated." In other words, according to Schweitzer, no
abiding principle for the guidance of Christians can
be found in this text and its parallels.[6] Whichever way
one would interpret the passage, it is clear that the
First Christian was Himself a realist and recognized
the facts in the case. Caesar's existence and that of
the Empire of which he was the head was a real fact
with which the individual Christian and the Church
itself must have to come to terms.

As soon as we get into the further passages of the
New Testament outside the Gospels we find rather
discordant testimony. St. Paul[7] would seem to teach
a doctrine of divine right of rulers practically unrestricted and apparently given the sanction of God's
own approval. It is further borne out by a curious
word in the Epistle to the Thessalonians:[8] "that which
restraineth." The early Pauline outlook saw in the
drama of world circumstance the evidence of God's
providence in operation: the law and order of Rome
were part and parcel of God's dispensation to mankind to the end of making His message of redemption
effective. On the other hand, in 1 Peter[9] we have a
different nuance: as the commentator has said about
the passage in contrast to the Pauline ideas, St. Peter
might have been the father of a political theory of
constitutional monarchy, while St. Paul could easily
have been quoted—as subsequently came to pass—
on the side of absolutism. The atmosphere of Johannine literature[10] is quite different. Here "the world"
—*Kosmos*—means society organized apart from God.
In the Apocalypse itself, that "Tract for Bad Times"
and "First Christian Statesman's Handbook," there

is entire antagonism between the Christian fellowship with its Lord on the one hand and the world and
its civilization, customs, culture, and laws on the
other.

The divergent views represented in New Testament
teaching then are prophetic of different estimates of
the relations between Church and State which came
subsequently to be believed and to be put into action.
The Dominical dictum is to be of paramount value,
but it may be interpreted in the Pauline, the Petrine,
or the Johannine sense. In other words, the "powers
that be" if "ordained of God" must be obeyed and
accepted; or "though they be ordained of God" may
be criticized and even repudiated; or there may be a
perpetual warfare between the Christian fellowship
and the civil or secular order. We shall find all of these
forms of interpretation furnishing fruitful standards
for Christian attitudes and action in the centuries to
come.

Perhaps the most characteristic passage reflecting
the attitude of the early Christian to the "world"
(which in fact means the Roman Empire) can be
found in the Epistle to Diognetus. "What the soul is
in the body that are Christians in the world. The soul
is dispersed throughout all the members of the body
and Christians are scattered through all the sections
of the world. The soul dwells in the body, yet is not of
the body; and Christians dwell in the world yet are
not of the world. (John xvii:11,14,16.) The invisible
soul is guarded by the visible body, and Christians
are known indeed to be in the world but their godli-
ness remains invisible. . . . The soul is imprisoned
in the body yet keeps that very body together; while

Christians are confined in the world as in a prison yet it is they who sustain the world. The immortal soul dwells in a mortal tabernacle; and Christians dwell as sojourners in that which is corruptible looking for incorruptibility which is in the heavens. . . . God has appointed them to so great a post and it is not right for them to decline it." (Epistle to Diognetus, vi.) All this harks back to the famous phrase of St. Paul in Philippians iii:20: "For we [Christians] are an outpost of Heaven," which means to say: the Christian fellowship is a bit of extra-territorial jurisdiction on earth of the world above.

These ideas controlled the constitution and belief of the early Christian Church in respect to its relation to the State. The two prepositions *in* but not *of* furnished as it were a succinct summary of the attitude the early believers had toward the whole of pagan domination. Elements of contradiction could be levelled down in the actual practice of a sufficient loyalty to the Empire and its head, the Caesar, despite persecution, martyrdoms, and exclusion from the full life of the secular world.[11] In a comparatively short time the Christian Church became an enclave in the Roman Empire, a kind of *imperium in imperio.* In that highly important document of St. Hippolytus, "The Apostolic Tradition," we have a good picture of typical third century Church life. The Church has now become an omnicompetent social organism, exercising a stringent moral authority over all its members, during the whole span of their lives from the cradle to the grave. Worship, edification, social life, benevolence and philanthropy are all included in the scope of the Christian community's consciousness.

One thing is very clear: primitive Christianity had little idea of a conversion of society as such. It confined its attention to saving individuals out of society *into* the *fellowship*. Hence it might be truly stated—so far as a generalization can convey truth—that Christians had little sense of social responsibility to the corporate whole of the pagan Empire and its culture and civilization.

The fourth century saw a devastating and catastrophic change both in the status and attitude of the Church. For about the same reasons that had actuated his predecessor Diocletian to seek in the last and worst of the persecutions to exterminate Christianity, Constantine sought to make Christians his allies. He did so under the same impulse and conviction and assumption that had animated his predecessors. As Eric Seeberg says: "In ancient fashion Constantine conceived the State and the exercise of religion to be one thing."[12]

The assumption that lay behind the whole of developed Roman rule was in brief that religion and patriotism were of the same piece. What we may think to be a rather modern invention, the totalitarian State, commonly so-called, flourished in the latter years of the Roman Empire. If there were one ruler there would of necessity be but one religion. The State could not tolerate a double loyalty. While it is true that the early pagan Roman Empire showed a remarkable degree of toleration for religions other than that of the State, this spirit had largely evaporated by the time when that transformation occurred, which turned the Roman Empire into what might be fitly described as an oriental despotism. It was this which the first Christian emperor inherited as the precedent and understood principle for his legislation. We have been accustomed to hear the word *Gleichschaltung* on the lips of Nazi protagonists as one of their great ideals. This same symbol of a program and policy directed the activities of the Christian emperors of the fourth century. Before the end of that century momentous legislation had taken place.[13] By this same time one of the most stubborn difficulties in its fulfilment also became apparent.

By the year 381 the government had ruled that Orthodoxy was a test of loyalty and that heresy was treason. It might be well to stop and consider this legislation. It is apparent that the assumption is "every loyal citizen must be in full agreement not only with regard to the laws and legislations of the government but also with its stand on religion." The conception thus so baldly stated derives from Jewish as well as from pagan sources. The ideal in the Old Testament as given by Ezekiel of a priest-king as head of a theocratic State is not essentially different from that of the pagan Empire. Later parallels may be found in the revolution of the Maccabees and the beginning of Pharisaism as a protest against the debasement of religion by its too intimate control on the part of the royal power. The same phenomenon is manifested by the steady protest of Christians against the dominance of the omnicompetent State over the affairs of Church and religion.[14] This theory of universal acceptance and conformity brought to light one very serious obstacle. This was due to the stubborn nationalism of minority groups in the fourth century Empire. In theory, the Empire was as universal as the

Church; in practice neither State nor Church immediately dealt successfully with the problem of insurgent nationalism.[15]

Constantine and his successors attempted to impose on civilization one rule, one culture, and one religion. The expression of all was in the almost universal common language of the world—Greek. While the pagan Empire had dealt wisely and constructively in coping with the small enclaves of people within the boundaries of the Empire, never insisting on anything but the minimum and willing to compromise or to accommodate save on matters of deepest principle, the Levantine rule from the New Rome on the Bosphorus either lacked the astuteness to carry on this policy or operated under the conviction of a different principle. Recent studies have demonstrated clearly that the so-called schismatic and heretical churches of the East which split off in the fourth and fifth centuries are chiefly to be considered as instances of a nationalist protest, ineffective and powerless in every other domain save that of religion, against the compulsory process of "one hundred percentism" emanating from Constantinople.[16]

Justinian's task at the outset of his reign was gigantic. What Constantine had so laboriously united suffered a process of erosion which bade fair to destroy totally the Roman Empire of the past with all its glamour and tradition. Insurgent and stubborn nationalist groups, barbarian invaders and colonists, and Persian aggressiveness gave him as a statesman a series of complex and apparently insoluble problems. Furthermore, the Church was in a rather discordant frame of mind and was honeycombed with alleged heretics and schismatics. The unitive principle of the State was the Roman law. The unitive principle of the Church was canonical and dogmatic law. It was genius on the part of Justinian to utilize Narses and Belisarius to reconquer lost territory in the West particularly, while buying off the Persians in the East. It was no less genius that he saw the high importance of the codification of classical Roman law. Here as well as in his letters we may best find the ideals which he set before him to be translated into institutions and social structure. My study has led me to isolate the following items as matters for special comment.

First of all, Justinian bent all his energies to the Christianization of the classic tradition of law. The age-long Roman law with its emphasis on order and justice derives from the very dawn of Roman history. It constitutes the greatest contribution that Rome has made to human life and civilization. The accumulated experience of the centuries went into it, but like all experience and the record thereof the formulations even of principle not to mention detailed legislation were in a chaotic state largely unintelligible to all but a very few experienced and aged men.[17] He had in view in his codification not only the simplification and clarification of classic Roman law but also the preparation of a universal handbook for generations of lawyers to come. Still more important was the recognition of a principle of definition and reapplication of the ancient rudiments to uncontemplated situations and unpredicted exigencies. But above all, Justinian's practical contribution was that he Christianized the old tradition of the past.

For this he had precedent going back to the *Audientia Episcopalis* of Constantine. The practical exemptions enjoyed by the clergy and the Church were over two centuries old. How recognize the existence of a supernatural society which owed its origin to God alone and a civil society which claimed no such divine authority? In other words, what was to be the basis for the relationship between Church and State? He asserted the principle that God had established two domains of authority among men, the crown and the priesthood. Both are mediators of divine authority and possess from the same source that position demanding man's allegiance which constitutes a religious obligation on the part of the loyal believer.[18] There is nothing actually new in the principle. What Justinian did was to give it coherent guarantee, precision and implementation. Roman law is now baptized and is a full member of the household of the Faith. The Church is the spiritual arbiter and moral judge of the law of justice that God had imparted to the Romans.[19]

Secondly, Justinian envisaged but one society, which was both Church and State at the same time. The aim of "justice" was the prime task of civil society and its ordering. More remote but basic was the conviction that the law of the State would have no other ultimate end in view than the chief aim which the Church proclaimed as her peculiar province: the living of human life in society with a view to doing God's will now and inheriting His gift of immortality hereafter. The far-reaching implications of the social ideal which Justinian set up are as effective in many quarters today as they were during his own lifetime. Let us examine this principle a little more closely. At bottom it is far distant from either the Pauline theory or that expressed in the Epistle to Diognetus to which I referred above. Back of it lies a whole conception as to Man and God. In the first place it is noteworthy that there is no pessimism here in Justinian's outlook on human nature. I might say at this point by way of parenthesis, that one of the most vital differences between the outlook of the East and that of the West is due to St. Augustine, whose view of mankind is far different from that assumed by Justinian and all the great theologians of Eastern Christendom. To Justinian, the secular was sacred and the sacred was secular. Just as man is constituted of body and soul, so the community is, so to speak, a common-unity. God is the author of both the temporal and the eternal, of both the material and the spiritual. The whole nexus of man's life has its two-fold reference for it has relations to time and space, or to the material and temporal and also becomes supremely significant as temporal and physical are necessarily and intimately related to the eternal. As Alivisatos points out, any denial or betrayal of religion would be of itself a betrayal of the State.[20] Gratian and Theodosius were equally clear on this point in legislation which it must be confessed seems to lack savor when tested by the modern appetite.

If it were true that matters of eternity and man's full solution of life in the world beyond the temporal were of final consequence; if it mattered what man did in time chiefly but not solely because of consequences yet to come beyond time, then the State had a just right to take cognizance of all such factors.

What we call Church and State (and for the more exact delineation of their real meanings we shall have to wait until a little later in our story), could not conceivably be set into opposition one to the other. Of necessity they are united. He conceived of society then as having this double reference—to time as well as to eternity. He could not conceive that the affairs having to do with the administration of the Empire, the correction of social abuses, the protection of the weak, and the multitude of concrete instances of all of these could be without their supernatural and eternal significance. The whole of Christian society was a unity. It was both the Church and the State combined.

A third item of interest in regard to the ideas which animated imperial legislation was the position of the Christian emperor in the scheme of things. Again, this position was consistent with the tradition out of which it logically grew. "Rightly has he been celebrated as a great emperor, since in the two tasks he set himself from the beginning he showed himself in fact as a great, yes, a very great emperor and even a greater bishop."[21] He conceived the royal power or the imperial authority to be given him by God. No less was he convinced that he had a practical task with reference to the Church. Again, to quote Alivisatos: "Justinian was convinced that he was both *imperator* and *pontifex maximus*, and his ecclesiastical legislation shows evidence of both offices, namely, that having to do with the Church and religion."[22] It is highly unfashionable today for us to think of the divine right of kings in any favorable light. As we shall see the story develop in the Middle Ages, for the understanding of it whether in the East or in the West, Justinian is indispensable. The theory of the divine right of kings has as its fundamental conviction what might be called the sacredness of the secular. Three attitudes can be adopted by the believing Christian with reference to civil society and the secular order: The order of civil society may be essentially indifferent religiously; or it may be hostile to the claims of Christianity; or it may be deemed sacred and holy by divine sanction. For example, with reference to this last, there need not be any great difference between the theory of the divine right of kings and the democratic dictum *vox populi, vox Dei*. Constantine had asserted that he was the bishop of the world, while the Christian bishops were only bishops in the Church.[23] Justinian acted on this principle in all his legislation. Not only was he a far better theologian[24] than most of the ecclesiastics of his time, not only did he exercise himself in nice points of doctrine and discipline, but he empowered the Church with authority effectively to exert the application of principles which it had asserted and formulated in the Church's councils. In a sense that cannot be gainsaid he was the head of the Church. He was not only its protector by reason of the fact that he preserved it from attack and fostered its activities, but even further: he forced the Christian fellowship to become aware of issues which might otherwise have been obscured or passed over in indifference. He exercised wide authority as to the appointment of bishops and the detailed regulations of Church life and customs. He invested with civil authority the hierarchy and gave them an extraordinary position even over judges, magistrates and governors.[25] He gave bishops tasks such as the receiving and spending of public moneys, the contracting and building of State edifices, bridges, wells, street-paving, water supply, as well as their repairs and restorations.[26] All benevolences were in the hands of the Church, the care of the sick, of widows and orphans, the infirm, and the needy. At every point he enforced belief in the ecumenical councils and the faith and practice of the orthodox Church.

Fourthly, in what I have just mentioned, I have suggested that he "enforced." Here I may fear the modern mind will find it difficult to understand and sympathize with Justinian's principles and methods. To put it quite baldly: the use of force against heretics, schismatics, unbelievers, Jews, and pagans, was written into the whole structure of Justinianic legislation. Two points here emerge: What is meant by this "establishment" of the Church? Is Christianity in any sense compatible with intolerance?

The most succinct definition of "establishment" involves the note of coercive authority superadded to the moral authority of the Church.[27] As in Italy's Concordat of July 1929, so in all other types of established religion the State supports with force that which the Church has decreed in canonical or moral law. There were not failing those who in the fourth and fifth centuries protested against the use of force in the matter of Christian conviction and behavior.[28] It must be admitted, however, that most of these voices were raised at the time when the persons or group which were making their protests articulate were themselves being subjected to force. In a later century that famous Anglican, Alcuin of York, protested energetically against Charles the Great's use of force in converting the Saxons.[29] Again, it may be pointed out that his attitude was not typical of his century any more than was that of St. Athanasius, St. Hilary of Poitiers in the fourth century, and others. His action brought to light this dilemma: if it is all important that the soul be saved and if salvation depends upon right belief, can force be exercised in compelling allegiance to the true faith, or, since faith is a free and voluntary act on the part of the believer, must force be left to one side?

This brings us to perhaps the most perplexing part of Justinian's scheme of things: his intolerance. We shall have to clear away a good deal of the brush of sentimentality and muddy thinking to find our way to a true realism of outlook. The easy optimism of modern man and that which he boasts of as his broad-mindedness and tolerance were foreign to the world of the West until long after the Reformation. What we call intolerance (and in so passing our verdict or judgment about it, condemn it) proceeds from some such combination of factors as the following: given the assumption that there is a right faith that it is necessary for every man to believe in order to inherit eternal salvation, and given the conviction that you possess this faith and have authority and power to make your will effective, how can there be any room for toleration? Pre-medieval and medieval Christianity were both sure that they had the true faith, all of it, without error. Just in proportion then as they valued it, and cared for the needs of human beings, many believers of this tradition became what we would call "persecutors." Furthermore, they had the wisdom to recognize that ideas are dangerous. If modern society can coop up a typhoid carrier or a person with active smallpox, thus denying his personal liberty with a view to the common good, on the assumption that matters of the spirit are even more important, and the right faith preeminently so, heretics were deemed dangerous elements in society; not only their action and spoken words, but even their presence constituted a challenge to what the majority recognized as vitally important and true. To understand either the medieval mind or the pre-medieval mind it is quite essential to enter with sympathy into an outlook so far different from our own. For the most part, we modern people of the twentieth century do not recognize the enormous importance of a right faith, or if we do are not quite sure we have it all, or if we are sure in this respect, we do not possess the power effectively to control and influence obedience and acceptance of what we believe to be true. There is a great deal of hypocrisy and cant disguising itself under the term "tolerance." Whatever we can find of the Christian life and ideals deriving from Justinian at least these two elements were notably lacking.[30]

From Justinian there came the inspiration, with certain modifications to be described later, of Charles the Great's Holy Roman Empire of the West. From him derive the social, political, or religious culture of the churches and peoples of Eastern Christendom. To this very day his ideas dominate the whole of the Near East and are matters to be reckoned with in any genuine world-outlook both on the political as well as on the religious side. Still more strange is it that the

English Reformation owed its directive principles to what he wrote and did. The tradition of Anglicanism would not have achieved its powerful and apparently paradoxical form had it not been for Justinian. The social structure of the whole of medieval life as well as a continuing influence within Protestant Christendom derive again from Justinian. It has seemed to me rather astonishing that so little attention has been given to a scientific study of what he attempted to achieve and what ideals prompted his achievement.[31]

[1] It may not be without interest to note the following points: In his *Restraint of Appeals Act* (24 Henry VIII 12; passed February 1533) the assertion is made: "That this Realm of England is an Empire and so hath been accepted in the world, governed by one supreme head and king, having the dignity and royal estate of the imperial crown of the same, unto whom a body politic compact of all sorts and degrees of people divided in terms and by names of spirituality and temporality, be bounden and ought to bear, also institute and furnished, by the goodness and sufferance of Almighty God, with plenary, whole, and entire power, preeminence, authority, prerogative and jurisdiction, to render and yield justice, and final determination to all manner of folk, residents, or subjects within this his realm, in all causes, matters, debates, and contentions, happening to occur, insurge, or begin within the limits thereof, without restraint, or provocation to any foreign princes or potentates of the world; the body spiritual whereof having power, when any cause of the law divine happened to come in question, or of spiritual learning, then it was declared, interpreted, and showed by that part of the said body politic, called the spirituality, now being usually called the English Church, which always hath been reputed, and also found of that sort, that both for knowledge, integrity, and sufficiency of number, it hath always thought, and is also at this hour, sufficient and meet of itself, without the intermeddling of any exterior person or persons, to declare and determine all such doubts, and to administer to such offices and duties, as to their rooms spiritual doth appertain; for the due administration whereof, and to keep them from corruption and sinister affection, the King's most noble progenitors, and the antecessors of the nobles of this realm have sufficiently endowed the said Church, both with honour and possessions." (Gee and Hardy, *Documents Illustrative of English Church History*, London, 1910, pp. 187-8.)

The Justinianic quality of this section is apparent, for Justinian divided society into the two parts or two sets of officials—the *regnum* and the *sacerdotium*. There is little doubt but that the King of England had read Justinian just before this was written. Furthermore, he abrogated the definition of heresy which had prevailed in Latin medieval canon law: "Et sciendum quod aliquis censetur hereticus multis modis. Is namque qui male sentit vel docet de fide, de corpore Christi, de baptismate, peccatorum confessione, matrimonio vel aliis sacramentis ecclesiae. Et generaliter qui de aliquo praedicto vel de articulis fidei aliter praedicat, docet, vel sentit quam doceat sancta mater ecclesia dicitor hereticus. . . . *Nam omnino censetur hereticus qui non tenet id quod docet et sequitur sancta romana ecclesia.* (Lyndwood, William, *Provinciale seu constitutiones Angliae . . .*, London, 1505, Lib. V, *De Hereticis*, Folio 157b.) What he strove to do was to take cognizance of all matters both of the State and of the Church in the spirit and according to the precedent of Justinian. Cf. Justinian's *Novellae*, 131, §a. (Lingenthal's edition, Part II, p. 267.) The canon law, the dogmas of the four ecumenical councils as well as

Holy Scripture were written into the civil legislation of the Justinianic Empire. At the time of that writing there were four ecumenical councils recognized. To this day the whole of the Anglican communion repeats the Justinianic phrase. In the Ten Articles of the year 1536 Justinian's influence is very apparent: "As touching the chief and principal articles of our faith . . . they ought and must most constantly believe and defend all those things to be true, which be comprehended in the whole body and canon of the Bible, and also in the three Creeds . . . and that they ought and must take and interpret all the same things according to the selfsame sentence and interpretation, which the words of the selfsame creeds or symbols do purport, and the holy approved doctors of the Church do entreat and defend the same. . . . Item, That they ought and must utterly refuse and condemn all those opinions contrary to the said Articles, which were of a long time past condemned in the four holy councils, that is to say, in the Council of Nice, Constantinople, Ephesus and Chalcedonense, and all other sith that time in any point consonant to the same."(Kidd, B. J., *The Thirty Nine Articles*, London, 1925, p. 13.)

Since Justinianic law was recognized and universally accepted by civil lawyers everywhere his canons were regarded as having a force of law. At the Diet of Augsburg in 1530 appeal was made to them by Cardinal Campeggio. (Justinian, *Code*, *Lib*. I, *Tit*. i, Lex. 4.) The law as incorporated into Justinianic legislation really goes back to the year after the Council of Chalcedon. Cardinal Campeggio is urging upon the emperor that imperial law as given by Justinian furnished him with quite effective authority to put down the Lutheran heresy. In so doing the legate and Cardinal Campeggio were urging the same standard of orthodoxy as that formulated by Justinian. Implicitly he is appealing to a far wider Catholic consent than would be the case in appealing to papal decretals, bulls, encyclicals, and the like. In short, the Justinianic influence both on the constitutional side (the Act "Restraint of Appeals" of 1533, cf. Gee and Hardy, *Documents*, pp. 187-95) and his further act forbidding papal dispensations and the payment of Peter's Pence (*ibid.*, 209 *ff.*) which may be described as the ecclesiastical program, prove the enormous importance of Justinian for the English Reformation. The same spirit is manifested in Elizabeth's Act of Supremacy of the year 1559 (Gee and Hardy, *Documents*, p. 455): "Provided always, and be it enacted by the authority aforesaid, that such person or persons to whom your highness, your heirs or successors, shall hereafter, by letters patent, under the great seal of England, give authority to have or execute any jurisdiction, power, or authority spiritual, or to visit, reform, order, or correct any errors, heresies, schisms, abuses, or enormities by virtue of this Act, shall not in anywise have authority or power to order, determine, or adjudge any matter or cause to be heresy, but only such as heretofore have been determined, ordered, or adjudged to be heresy, by the authority of the canonical Scriptures, or by the first four general Councils, or any of them, or by any other general Council wherein the same was declared heresy by the express and plain words of the said canonical Scriptures, or such as hereafter shall be ordered, judged, or determined to be heresy by the High Court of Parliament of this Realm, with the assent of the clergy in their Convocation; anything in this Act contained to the contrary notwithstanding."

² Overall, John, Bishop of Norwich, 1560-1619, *Bishop Overall's Convocation Book MDCVI Concerning the Government of God's Catholic Church and the Kingdoms of the Whole World*, London, 1690.

³ *op. cit.*, Preface.

Matt. xxii:21. The Dominical statement rested upon the Jewish tradition.

⁴ Deut. xvii:15 reads "Thou must not put a foreigner over thee who is not thy brother." Cf. the words of Judas the Gaulonite in Josephus' *Antiquities*, XVIII, I.1; Theudas, *ibid.*, XX, V. 1; Eleazar: "We will not serve the Romans or any man; only God alone." (*Bell. Jud.*, VII, viii, 6.) There were different Jewish views as represented by the different schools of thought within Judaism. The Rabbinic Prayer of Thanksgiving on seeing a King expresses the sense of the divinely derived authority he possesses: "Blessed art Thou, O God, Ruler of the Universe, who hast imparted Thy Majesty to flesh and blood." (Ber., 58ᵃ; 20 Bar.) Again: "He who rebels against the King is as he who rebels against the divine presence." (*Shekina*; Bereshit, R. 60ᵃ.) A third century rabbi casts the same favorable verdict on civil and secular authority: "The law of the kingdom is [God's] law." (Baba Kama, 113ᵃ.) The Rabbinic theory might be stated as: "Whosesoever coin passes current his rule is accepted." (Baba Kama, IX:2.) Besides these opinions the zealots or Cananaeans were unmitigatedly hostile to the Roman rule, just as the Sadducee opinion was slavishly uncritical of it and thoroughly loyal.

It might be interesting to turn our attention briefly to some of the typical Patristic interpretations of the Dominical maxim. Origen: "Because a man renders unto Caesar the things that belong to Caesar it is no hindrance to him in rendering to God what belongs to God."

Tertullian, *De Idol.*, 15, comments on the passage in the words: "That is, the image of Caesar is money, the image of God is man. Give money to Caesar, and give thyself to God."

St. John Chrysostom says: "What does no harm to piety or religion pay. The tribute or toil which is opposed to virtue and the faith is the tribute or revenue of the Devil."

St. Hilary of Poitiers supplements his commentary with the words: "If we have nothing in our possession which belongs to Caesar then are we free of the obligation of giving him what is his."

St. Ambrose is too long to quote but in the year 386 he preached a sermon against Auxentius of which sections 22, especially 31-32 and his Epistles 40, 41, 51, are particularly relevant.

⁵ Compare parallels Mark xii:17; Luke xx:25.

⁶ Schweitzer, Albert, *The Quest of the Historical Jesus, a Critical Study of its Progress from Reimarus to Wrede*, London, A. C. Block, 1910.

⁷ cf. Rom. xiii:1-7 on which Bigg (*ICC*, p. 39) says: "A doctrine of divine right could be built on the words of St. Paul and not upon those of St. Peter." Cf. Sanday and Headlam 14th ed., New York, 1913. (*ICC*, pp. 365-72, Excursus.)

[8] cf. 2 Thess. ii:1-7. Furthermore, the Pastorals inculcate the duty of prayer for the King. 1 Tim. ii:1-2; Titus iii:1. The same feeling appears in 1 Clement, 60-1; and the Epistle of Polycarp *ad Phil.*, 12.

[9] cf. 1 Pet. ii:13 *ff.* and Bigg's comment, *loc. cit.*

[10] cf. 1 John xvii: 1 John iii: 2; John xv-xvii; also Dr. Charles' "Commentary on the Apocalypse" in *ICC*, Vol. I, p. ciii: "While the Seven Churches represent entire Christendom, Rome represents the power of this world. With its claims to absolute obedience, Rome stands in complete antagonism to Christ. Between these two powers there can be no truce or compromise. . . . The Apocalypse is thus the divine statute book of international law. In this spirit of splendid optimism the seer confronts the world-power of Rome with its blasphemous claims to supremacy over the spirit of man."

[11] The literature of the Apologists is instructive. Melito of Sardis in his *Apologia* addressed to Marcus Aurelius says: "Our doctrine flourished for the good of the Empire." Athenagoras states boldly: "We are piously disposed toward God and your government," and in Apollonius' *Apology*, he says: "We too love the emperor and offer our prayers for his majesty." On the other hand, after the turn into the third century, the discipline represented by the Apostolic Tradition of St. Hippolytus gave to the government no possible compliance. Among the classes of people who cannot be received as catechumens are "A soldier of the civil authority . . . a military commander or civil magistrate that wears the purple must resign or be rejected. If a catechumen or a believer seeks to become a soldier they must be rejected for they have despised God." (Easton, Burton Scott, *The Apostolic Tradition of St. Hippolytus*, Cambridge University Press, 1934, p. 40.)

[12] Seeberg, Eric, "Die Synode Von Antiochien im Jahre 324/25," in *Neuen Studien zur Geschichte der Theologie und der Kirche*, Berlin, 1913, Vol. XVI, p. 194.

[13] *Theodosian Code Book*, p. 7. *Lib.* XVI, *Tit.* V, 6, Laenel's edition, 1840. Cols. 1525-7.

[14] cf. Hilary of Poitiers' *First Epistle to Constantius* of the year 355, his *Second* to the same in the year 359, and his *Invective* against Constantius. Hosius of Cordova writes to Constantius (355): "Intrude not yourself into ecclesiastical matters, neither give commands unto us concerning them, but learn them from us. God hath put into your hands the kingdom; to us he hath entrusted the affairs of his Church. . . . By taking on yourself the governance of the Church you become guilty of a great offense. It is written 'Render unto Caesar'. . . . Neither is it permitted unto us to exercise an earthly rule nor have you any authority to burn incense." Cf. also St. Athanasius, *Hist. Arianorum*, IV, 43-4.

[15] Woodward, Ernest Llewellyn, *Christianity and Nationalism in the Early Roman Empire*, Longmans Green, 1916.

[16] cf. Woodward, *op. cit.*

[17] cf. second century texts on the history of Roman law. *Corpus iuris Romani anteiustinani*, Böcking, Bonn, 1840.

[18] *Novella* VI in Lingenthal's edition, Part I, Leipzig, 1881, XII, pp. 44-5.

[19] It might be plausibly urged that what Justinian did was to reduce Christianity to a new legalism. If he actually did so his action was not without precedent; the tendency so to do is clear in the First Gospel, and in the First Epistle of Clement to the Corinthians, where the essential element in his argument is "Learn to subject yourself" (c. 57.2), and the solid tradition which on the whole is characteristic of early Roman Christianity. In exalting and repristinating the ideal of justice, Justinian, as had some of his Christian predecessors, maintained the correlative Christian principle of love. The two constitute as it were the warp and woof of the full garment of divinely given imperial authority. Justinian could no more have conceived of a Christian principle that was not embodied in practice and institutions than he could have thought of Christian faith existing in a precarious no-man's land of the sheer ideal, unrelated and unincorporated and unapplied. Practical motives were as potent to him as idealistic.

[20] Alivisatos, Hamilcar, "Die kirchliche Gesetzgebung des Kaisers Justinian I," in *Neue Studien zur Geschichte der Theologie und der Kirche*, Vol. XVII, p. 6.

[21] *op. cit.*, p. 7.

[22] *ibid.*, p. 121.

[23] Eusebius, *Vita Constantini*, xxiv.
"He too said he was a bishop: you are bishops with a jurisdiction inside the Church: 'I also am a bishop ordained of God to oversee whatever is external to the Church.' . . . For he watched over his subjects with an episcopal care and exhorted them to follow a godly life."
Socrates, *H. E.*, V, Intro. "Wherever the affairs of the State were disturbed, those of the Church (as if by some vital sympathy) were disturbed also. . . . From the time the emperors began to profess the Christian religion, the affairs of the Church have depended on them so that even the greatest synods have been and still are convened by their appointment." Compare also Sozomen, *H. E.*, I, 19: "Constantine passed through to the head of the conference [Nicaea] and seated himself on the throne which had been prepared for him, and the synod was then commanded to be seated."

[24] Compare, for example, his Epistle on the *Three Chapters*, where the acumen and insight he demonstrates quite incidentally and casually constitutes the document of conspicuous moment in sixth century theological exploration and attainment.

[25] *Code*, 1.3.44; also *Nov.*, 131.18, *Mar.*, 545, Lingenthal's edition, Part II, Leipzig, 1881, pp. 266 *ff.* In paragraph 1 he makes imperial law to include the canons of the four ecumenical councils—Nicaea, Constantinople, Ephesus, and Chalcedon, saying that the dogmas of such synods like Holy Scripture and their canons are to be preserved as law.

[26] *Code*, 1.4.26.

[27] cf. Mirbt, Carl, in *Encyclopedia Britannica*, eleventh edition, Vol. XIX, p. 640: "According to Gelasius in his *Historia Concilii Nicaeae*, II, 33, 'Nicaea' admitted the principle that the State might employ the secular arm to bring the Christian subjects of the Roman world empire under the newly codified faith." See also Grupp in *The Catholic Encyclopedia*, IV, p. 299, s.v. *Con-*

stantine. A little later Vegetius, *de re militari*, II, 5, is quoted by Hodgkin in *The Dynasty of Theodosius*, Oxford, 1889, pp. 36-7: "For that man, whether soldier or civilian serves God, who faithfully loves him who reigns by God's ordinance. . . . For when the emperor receives the name of Augustus, faithful and incessant devotion is to be shown him as to God present in the flesh, and lifelong service is to be paid him."

²⁸ See note 14 above.

²⁹ Alcuin says: "Apart from faith what is the use of baptism? . . . Faith must come freely and not under duress. How can a man be forced to believe what he does not actually believe? While a man may be coerced into being baptized yet can he not be forced into the faith" (cf. *M. G. H.* Ep. IV, 174).

³⁰ Our ancestors reasoned somewhat as follows: Justice means granting to everyone his due—to God worship and obedience; to man what is rightly his worth by virtue of the title of his fundamental humanity or of his actual achievement. The obligation of justice as a right relationship to both God and man must be squarely put before every single believer even were he to shrink from accepting the obligations so presented. What was best for him—even though he knew it not and failed to appreciate the fact—must if necessary be forced on him for the threefold reason that justice demanded that God be properly served, that the fellowship be not harmed and endangered, and that the individual person in question know justice as eternal salvation. Even the law of charity could be invoked to supplement the law of justice; the kindest thing that a physician can do to one in grave physical danger from accident or disease is to insist as pressingly as possible upon the patient's undergoing what might appear to be far more painful a method of therapy than the alternative, to leave the situation alone. Pain and suffering may prove the only possible method of restoration to health. Christian loving-kindness might appear—as it did frequently in history—as harsh and austere. Many times of course it is obvious that this sense of responsibility as well for God, for society, and for the individual was but a rationalization of a desire for dominance. In the main, however, there is a wholesome side—granted the way in which people scheduled their table of values and ordered their behavior-patterns congruent thereto, even to what we denominate persecution and intolerance. The fundamental points of reference as to the ordering of the whole human life—its perspective, its aim, and the necessary means thereto are vastly different in this modern world of ours from what they were in the age of Justinian.

³¹ cf. Baker, G. P. A., *Justinian and Constantine*, New York, 1931. pp. xvii-340. Also Holmes, W. G., *The Age of Justinian and Theodora*, 2 vols., London, 1907.

cf. his Sixth Novella of the year 535: "Concerning the ordination of bishops and presbyters and deacons, men and women, and of what sort should be the discipline for those who trangress the prescriptions laid down." The Novella is a letter from the Emperor Justinian to "Epiphanios, the Most Holy Archbishop of this royal city and Ecumenical Patriarch." The opening passage is of particular significance in that it states so clearly the distinction between *imperium* and *sacerdotium.* I quote: "The greatest of those gifts of God among men given from God's great love for man are the priesthood and secular authority. For the former ministers to the things of God and the latter rules over and cares for the things of man; each proceeds from the one and selfsame origin for the decent ordering of human life, in such fashion that nothing should be more dear to Emperors than the probity of the priests who beseech God always for them. For if the priesthood be always and everywhere blameless and is constituted of those who share in the right of free access to God, and rightly and properly order the life of the kingdom associated with it, then there will be an adequate concord bestowing upon the human race every possible good thing. We have then the greatest possible zeal concerning both the true dogmas of God as well as the probity of the priests." (Lingenthal's edition, Leipzig, 1881, Part I, No. xii, pp. 44-5.)

For an extremely modern parallel compare the Manifesto of His Beatitude Alexander III in reference to the consecration of His Grace, Antony Bashir for America, on April 19, 1936, and given at Beirut on the 5th day of January, 1937:

"God Almighty; blessed be His holy name and His glorious gifts, has ordered for this world two systems of ruling and willed it to be governed by two authorities; first the worldly authority, which He gives to whomsoever he wants, and to this the Holy Apostle referred by saying 'Let every soul obey and fear.' The second authority is the divine order [priesthood] which was ordered by our Lord and Saviour Jesus Christ in His Holy Church and is superior to the worldly authority in the same measure that the spirit is superior to the flesh and the immortal to the mortal. For the worldly authority is temporal and spatial, but this [the divine priesthood] is infinite and limitless because it deals with the necessary things for salvation, namely the Holy and Divine Sacraments given us by the Source of Life, Our Saviour Jesus Christ, without which none may inherit the Kingdom of Heaven."

II

MEDIEVAL DELIMITATION OF THE TWO POWERS: EARLIER PERIOD

THE IDEALS OF CHARLES THE GREAT

THE only figure in the West who occupies anything of the same importance as Justinian did to the East is that of Charles the Great.[1] The ideals of the Holy Roman Empire as formulated by him become institutionalized and lasted down to the Great War. Alcuin tells us that he constantly had St. Augustine's *De Civitate Dei* at hand for ready reference and frequent reading.[2] It is the effect of this Augustinian influence which distinguishes his, most sharply from Justinian's scheme of civilization and gave the Saint of Hippo that unique position in the Western Christian world which he has not failed to maintain until this present.

In his brilliant posthumous work, Dr. Figgis traces out in some detail the political importance of *De Civitate Dei*.[3] To him we are indebted not only for a shrewd criticism of Augustinian thought but also for the keen analysis of the great Father's meaning that lay behind the writing of this work. St. Augustine is not talking about the "City" of God, but about two rival societies: the one organized without reference to God—that of this world—and that of the other which is entirely subordinated to His will. The easiest deduction would be to identify God's *Civitas* with the Church, and to identify the other *Civitas* with the

State. In fact, most commonly this deduction has been drawn from the days of Charles the Great, to the great detriment of the preservation of the richness of Augustinian thinking and to its inevitable misapplication. Basically, Charles the Great sought to do for the West what Justinian sought to do for the East. The great difference lay in the outlook on human nature which Augustine had brought into Western thought. As over against the robust optimism of the Eastern tradition in general and in particular, a certain healthy skepticism about the nature of man and his aspirations marked the structure and scope of Carolingian society. Although St. Augustine has never been to the East an authority of first magnitude; the same Father has been for the West uniquely important and dominant in his influence, even when misinterpreted, comparable only to St. Paul.

Along with Justinian, Charles the Great thought of the head of society as being the Christian Prince. In him as the coordinating member and head of this society is the lodgment of sovereignty. Theoretically, spiritual independence is given the Church under its head the Pope. Practically, however, the Pope was subordinate to the Emperor. Charles the Great came to be an emperor from the status of having been only a king; and plenary jurisdiction and authority therefore belonged to him as a right. It was God-given authority which created the imperial dignity as well as the papal. The Justinianic twofoldedness of *imperium* and *sacerdotium* appears throughout the scheme of things as outlined by Charles. From Charles the Great derives that conception of the relation of Church and State which was to govern the Middle Ages in the West. As Dr. Figgis has pointed out elsewhere Church and State from the ninth century on in the West meant two sets of officials of this same single society. Many remnants of this conception remain even now in English usage. For example: When a young man is ordained, he is said to "enter the Church"; the word "Churchman" has until latterly meant ecclesiastic. As is obvious, this conception of one single unified society of which the ecclesiastical corporation formed the soul and the civil order the body, is much older than Justinian. Its roots really go back to Ezekiel's doctrine of a theocratic king, but this was elastic and patent of a wide interpretation and modification in the course of the early Christian centuries. The ideal enshrined in the Carolingian edifice of the Holy Roman Empire is its continuator, and even Machiavelli's *Prince* is in direct line of succession from Charles' ideal of the Christian ruler.

Augustinian pessimism, and a certain skeptical underestimation of human capacity made chemical combinations of entirely new forms with the solid tradition derived from Justinian and the East. Where Justinian did expect the bishops to be secular judges, their bench to be the supreme court of appellate jurisdiction, their council to be of primary authority, Charles the Great, on the contrary, utilized the episcopate in the fashion of those later rulers of the West whose ministers and chief magistrates were taken from the Church.[4]

The oversight given to ecclesiastical affairs by Charles the Great was tremendous. He asserted precisely the same authority in Church matters as he did in those of the State, with the same detail and scope of his interests in control. He was no less interested in liturgical reform, for example, than in securing the Pope's approval of his nominations to various bishoprics; no less keen for both political and religious reforms, for the conversion of heretics to Catholicism, than he was in the raising of the standard of education for the clergy and the disciplining of them for ecclesiastical offenses.[5] He believed in a forthright fashion in what St. Augustine rather reluctantly admitted— the use of coercion in converting non-Christians and non-believers as well as heretics to an acceptance of the Catholic Faith.[6] The difference here lay in the fact that Augustine could not advocate this technique whole-heartedly; to Charles the Great it seemed right both in principle and practice. It is the sturdy Alcuin who has the temerity to protest with vigor and to try to maintain the point that the essence of Christianity was its voluntary and free acceptance on the part of the believer.[7] War, education, reorganization of society, the prescriptions of economic and political procedure and law—all these were allegedly incorporated into a huge system of law and statute, all serving the same end as that which Justinian had proposed—the thoroughgoing Christianization of the whole of the life of man in all its relationships.

The civilization which Charles was in the way of creating was an entirely new brand. The Greek tradition of Justinian came forth as the Roman law and ideal. It was Rome who was the mistress of law, and Roman Christianity which was the Christianization of that law. After all, Constantinople was New Rome, and Justinian was preeminently a "Roman" emperor. A curious survival of this attitude exists in colloquial Greek and Turkish today where "Roman" equals what we mean by Greek.[8] Charles the Great claimed to be what the Greeks would term *basileus* expressed to mean "emperor," while the term in common parlance is thought of in the schools to mean king. As Emperor of the West his title, so far as the East was concerned, would seem a matter of impudent arrogation. To him it was that symbol which would consolidate the diversified traditions which were to make for the building of modern Europe. The Latin tradition was hardly distinguishable from what we would call the Greek tradition; the common law was that of Justinian, the Emperor of New Rome, whose title read: "The Autocrat Caesar Flavian Justinian, the Most Revered Augustus." On the other hand, there was the new incorporation of the Anglo-Saxon and Teutonic elements with their sturdy and stubborn usages and ingrained mental attitudes in some fashion to be combined with the classical stream emanating both from the best in pagan Latin and Greek thought as well as its Christianized reformulation. For example, kingship could in essence not be so much hereditary and inherited as constituted by proper election. Within a few years of Charles' death the controversy arose between curialist and imperialist. Two accounts of his life and works, one from each of these two sides tell different stories, and make different claims. Neither side, however, begrudges the main principle: Essential culture and social reorganization for the West would be at once Latin-Greek, and also Teutonic, and in all cases what was projected as well by curialist as well as imperialist was one single unitary society with the Emperor in a unique position at its top while the Pope had the domain of ecclesiastical affairs as his unique prerogative.

GREGORY THE SEVENTH

Gregory VII, who for twenty years before becoming Pope had been the power behind the papal throne, was a spiritual son of St. Augustine.[9] It would be out of the question here to try to develop as a whole his teaching and philosophy. What concerns us chiefly is what he thought about Church and State and their relationship, and the only point of departure that would really lead us into the heart of the matter comes from St. Augustine. It is significant enough to quote this passage which more than any other epitomizes Gregory's views. It comes from the *De Civitate Dei*, IV, 4—"If justice be put to one side what are kingdoms save instances of robbery on a large scale? For that matter, what are robberies more than kingdoms on a small scale? For military force itself is of man, and ruled by the power of the prince, is bound together by a social pact, and spoil is divided by a law which meets the common will. This is evil when, however, it grows by gradual degrees in the society of unregenerate men—so that it takes possession of places, sets up rule, captures cities, subjugates peoples, assumes for itself very openly the name of 'kingdom' but obviously it is true that cupidity has not been done away with, but in addition there has come impunity. For quite practically and in accordance with facts, a certain pirate captured by Alexander the

Great gave reply to the latter. And when this same king asked the man how it seemed to him that he should be such a scourge on the sea he replied with daring boldness: that it seemed so, said he, to you as a king of the whole world; but because I do this with a very small boat I am called a pirate; because you do it with a great fleet you get the name of emperor."

Back of Gregory VII's letter to Hermann of Metz, March 15, 1081, of which the title is "Against those who foolishly say that the emperor cannot be excommunicated by the Roman pontiff" stands this line of reasoning. Let me quote from this document: "Who is ignorant of the fact that kings and rulers have obtained their authority from those who in ignorance of God, actually under the impulse of the Prince of this World, the Devil, through pride, rapine, perjury and murders, in fact by almost all types of wickedness have come to dominate over their own equals, that is, their fellowmen, in blind greed and unbearable pride."[10] To Gregory, the story was perfectly clear. The order of civil society, of law and discipline, of the organization of the political and economic structure, was most emphatically of this world and not of God. It had no title or claim—save that of force or at the least of necessity—to the obedience and allegiance of Christian men. Only one thing could redeem it. The whole of society had to be baptized, must needs be put into subjection to the supernatural society of the Church, and the authority thus given shall derive solely from the spiritual order. Civil society, social, economic, and political life had in themselves no warrant or rightful title deserving of either respect or obedience. Only when the Church was in complete control of society could the latter rightfully claim the allegiance of the Christian man.

An analogy immediately springs to mind. Theoretically at least, the Middle Ages saw philosophy solely as the handmaid of theology. The implication in both cases is fairly clear—possibly far more so in the latter than in the former instance. If man's reason was capable of salvation by being controlled by revelation, then despite the gloomy and pessimistic outlook of both St. Augustine and St. Gregory VII, the State and all its works and ways were at least susceptible of this conversion. And what is thus capable of being changed must have something within it of the persistently good quality potentially something better than it was. There is therefore in both the Augustinian and Gregorian pessimism some hope, nay more, assurance of the redemption of society and of the political order. It was realism which dictated in both cases—St. Augustine's as well as St. Gregory's—the historical interpretation through which arose their pessimism with regard to the State. When he wrote his *De Civitate Dei*, St. Augustine was writing about the ideal Christian society, and not a city; it was about a civilization that *should be* rather than what *was*; it was about an order of life in the State and in social and economic life which would meet with God's approval,[11] in high contrast to the reality of the experiences of the fifth century. This same situation created the background for St. Gregory's views. Few men have been so unsuccessful in what they did so far as concerned the days in which they lived, and few men have been more conspicuously effective both as to what they did and what they said, with reference to the verdict of posterity.[12]

The two chief objectives which Gregory set himself were the fight against married clergy and the attempt to do away with what he called "simony." By the latter term was meant exercise on the part of laity of their *jus patronatus* in the form of investing with the symbols of authority ecclesiastics who were also great feudal landlords. It is perhaps pointless to remark that the word simony had strayed widely from its original and its secondary connotation, for what the term means in itself is the purchase of spiritual gifts. We may see in both of these ideas of St. Gregory the attempt to free the Church from the State, especially from the feudal State. In so doing, it has been well said of him that he set up a rival feudalism. Economically and socially it was necessary to free the clergy from those bonds of social life which are involved by family relations. Throughout the Middle Ages, while the theory was held strictly in official quarters the practice was only intermittently observed: innumerable instances can be shown of the inheritance by the priest's oldest son not only of the parish but of many of the items of the Church's actual equipment. Were the State or the secular order to have such power over the personnel of the Church as to be able through social, economic, or political pressure to control it—either by way of the clergymen whose family and their future mattered deeply to him or by way of investiture of the higher clergy by representatives of the ruling class—no way of independence of the Church from the State seemed feasible. In fighting feudalism Gregory in fact created a feudal state of the Church in place of a feudalized Church within the State.

Latin theology has always made much of the two aspects of the Church, which the Eastern tradition has always denied: *Ecclesia docens et ecclesia discens.* This is truly Gregorian for it is a matter of great moment that the hierarchy actually constitute the positive and affirmative side of the Church. This usage has even passed over into the common English tradition.

For all practical purposes to Gregory the Church was the clergy. The Middle Ages, in short, show us from his time on the clash of an institution or rather the institutionalizing of what had grown and under Gregory's impulse assumed fixed form, in which the clergy were the Church. The laity were those whose duty it was to obey and serve. The laity, that is, *ecclesia discens*, would take an ell if they could get an inch, according to St. Gregory. Therefore their pastoral function was to be taught, to be directed: if one were to conjugate medieval ecclesiastical history, it would be the clergy in the active and the laity in the passive voice.

Now it is perfectly true that much of this tradition was inherited by Hildebrand, but it is equally true that it is due to him that it received the formulation which imprinted upon it by his powerful mind, has been potent throughout subsequent history in Western Christendom. When one examines the history of the eleventh century it is hard not to feel a great sense of sympathy with Hildebrand. As history so often does, a dilemma was posed to the leaders of the Church and of State alike, the necessity of which, at least as one views it in retrospect, was not inevitable. Some other formulation might have been provided. Historical exigency is responsible for many conditions, much theorizing, and not a few cases of antitheses which in their own nature are not necessarily mutually exclusive. In doing battle with medievalism, as we have noted above, Gregory VII created a feudal ecclesiastical State of the Church, which for the Latin West has been the dominating tradition from his time on until this present. Now shorn of its past temporal riches, the papacy must still needs have an independent State no matter how small. The concordat of June 1929 is entirely in the mind of Gregory. A purely spiritual official, as one would deem the ecclesiastic to be, might not seem to need a temporal State in which to live independently. That this is more apparent than real may appear from a further consideration of the subject.

The Christian Church is two things at once—an alleged supernatural institution founded by Christ, but also composed of human beings, incorporated as a society holding property, living in time and space, and, insofar as it is in touch with its own age and the popular mind, largely swayed at any given moment by contemporary thought and opinion as well as conditioned by actualities of concrete conditions and the climate of political and social life. A purely "spiritual" corporation the Christian Church has never been. From the earliest days, as one reads in the New Testament, its officials concerned themselves with matters of money and food, the redirection of social custom and the ideals and creation of behavior-patterns. From the very beginning, Christianity has affirmed itself to be hostile to any type of dualism which would contrast and make mutually antagonistic the so-called spiritual and the so-called material. Insofar as the Christian Church is a supernatural corporation it does not need to be a property holder nor would it seem to need to concern itself with matters in the political and economic order. But insofar as the supernatural order is not regarded as in antagonism but rather complementary to the natural, all the activities of men are subsumed under the sway of the Church. As has been suggested, St. Augustine's formulation gave a certain twist to the Western conception and interpretation of these ideas by which— quite unlike the Eastern approach—the civil and social organization of the natural man came to be regarded as not only inadequate but as we have been seeing from St. Gregory positively vicious. So extensive would be the rule of an omnicompetent Church that there would be nothing outside the purview of its interests or activities. Until the conflict between the Church and the State arose to its climax in the Middle Ages in the West, and even during that conflict the great politicians (by which I mean students of politics and political thinkers) were ecclesiastics.[13] The process of development from Gregory through Innocent III[14] and Boniface VIII on up through Trent and the Vatican Council of 1870 would seem to be continuous.

Some interesting deductions derive from Gregory's ideas. If all the social and political policies of mankind are in their nature wrong in origin and only become right by being securely under the control of the Church, then it is a matter of indifference under what form of social order men live. Autocratic tyranny, constitutional monarchy, democracy, and any other conceivable political and social organization would all rest under the same condemnation. So as a matter of practice, it has been very easy for many ecclesiastics of the West, having St. Gregory's views in mind, to be entirely indifferent as to which of the alternative forms of political organization might be nearer the mind of Christ. One cannot but feel that the hierarchic feudal organization of the Church of the West under one supreme ruler would find more congenial a form of political and social life in which one ruled alone, supreme and absolute who must be dealt with.[15]

As is often the case in controversy when the two parties to it lock in conflict, what conditioned Gregory's restatement of the Latin Church's position of the West was the actuality of political and historical exigency. In order to overcome a feudalized State he created a feudalized Church. That this is true not only of political and ecclesiastical theory but as well of theological thought may be easily seen by review of St. Anselm's *Cur Deus Homo*. This glorious interpretation of the Atonement uses the ideal of feudalism no less than did St. Gregory when he expounded his theory of the relation between Church and State. Of St. Anselm it might be mentioned, in passing, that the more effective a piece of apologetic, the more ephemeral it must of necessity be. St. Anselm came to grips with the great problem of the Incarnation and Atonement in the strict idiom of his own time and in accordance with the assumptions in the minds of his readers. St. Gregory's adaptation of secular feudalism to the supernatural Church was a parallel instance of the same insight, and may be so far deplored in that it interprets Christian society in the vein of feudalism.

In a feudal state the secular side of the Church life would necessarily have to be feudal. But with consummate clarity of conviction Gregory kept the Church free by his twofold policy from the worst evil of feudalism—namely a kind of Confucian caste system. It was strictly true that for the greater part of the Middle Ages—as it has been since—the one escape from a fixed social and economic order was the Church. A boy of very humble antecedents could become a cardinal and even Pope. Neither poverty nor lack of family connections stood in the way of ability. In this respect, feudalize the Roman Church as he did, Gregory saved it from the curse of the sterilization of opportunity.

It is difficult to see in his writings that he distinguished between the Church as a supernatural society and the Church as an institution in time and space. The same would hold for the illustrious founder of the counter-reformation of a religious order which possibly more than any other single community of regulars in the Roman Church has sustained and promoted the Gregorian ideal. St. Ignatius Loyola's counsel to defend every single institution and usage of the Church, in the form in which he expounds it in the *Spiritual Exercises*,[16] is of the same spirit as that of St. Gregory. If the Church were itself a State, in fact *the State*, part of whose task it would be to control every State of whatever sort, pass judgment upon and guide the rulers of the secular State, then there must needs be powerful divine sanctions for the claim that this envisages. In the Dictatus Papae[17] which were possibly formulated a few years before Gregory's letter to Hermann of Metz certain statements are set down which would illustrate this further theory. For example, No. 8: "That only the Pope can use the imperial insignia." No. 9: "That princes alone should kiss the feet of the Pope." No. 12: "That to him solely belongs the power to depose emperors." No. 27: "That it is possible to absolve from their oaths of loyalty the subjects of unrighteous rulers." Again he says in the famous treatise written to Hermann of Metz: "But if kings are to be judged with regard to their sins by priests, by whom more rightly than by the Roman pontiff should they be judged?"[18] The struggle which was to last for centuries between Church and State may therefore begin with Otto the Great,[19] at least potentially, but actually its first overt instance would be the conflict between Gregory and Henry IV.

From Gregory on throughout the whole of the Middle Ages we must keep closely in mind that Church and State meant something quite different to them then than they mean to us in modern times. To us the Church and State are two different organizations. As we saw in the case of Justinian and in the ideal laid down by Charles the Great, there was to be one unified order both spiritual and temporal in which the Church was the soul and the State the body. Therefore, as Figgis pointed out "Church" and "State" mean two sets of officials of the same society not two rival organizations. For whether we deal with the East or with the West in the Middle

Ages such an innovation as the separation of Church and State would be unthinkable. Church in short means churchman, that is, ecclesiastic; State means statesman, that is, the officials of the political order. Again, by implication Gregory helped formulate and clarify this comparison though he did not create it.[20]

In the exhaustive study by Dr. Carl Mirbt (*Die Publizistik zur Zeitalter Gregors VII*, Leipzig, 1894), his painstaking analysis of documents and sources, both for and against Gregorianism as well during as after his pontificate, constitutes an authoritative monument of scholarship indispensable to the student of the period. He points out among other matters that the tendency of the writers was to cloak themselves in anonymity, by which device they secured a more favorable reception of their ideas, avoided the overt hostility of their opponents, and achieved some objective consideration of their respective arguments apart from personal elements.[21] He says that of the bishops who wrote, nearly two-thirds were Italians[22] and that there were approximately sixty-five works and monographs on the Gregorian side to fifty for the opposition, during the lifetime of Gregory. After his death there were thirty-six in favor of his policies to twenty-eight against them.[23] He discusses the significance of the twofold campaign of Gregory—for compulsory celibacy of the clergy and against simony.[24] The expedient of calling in lay opinion in the course of his campaign receives due attention.[25] From another point of view Fliche in his *La réforme Grégorienne* traverses somewhat the same territory. So significant are the words of Mirbt near the conclusion of his volume that I should wish to quote them more or less at length: "The writers on both sides were animated by the conviction that Church and State had to cooperate. This mutual understanding between the two powers was highly valued, and it was expected that not only mutual esteem but reciprocal love should characterize the relationship, inasmuch as both Church and State had a common task in leading the nation towards the achievement of divinely set ends in the prosecution of which they stood in need of each other so as to justify themselves in the light of these aims. Both powers had to preserve friendly relations in order to secure the well-being of both Church and State. Whenever and so long as hostile tension divided them, both would be circumscribed in the effective working out of their respective functions. That there were essential differences between the two powers and their peculiar provinces and aims was in no sense denied. A recognition of the fact that the State was under obligation to protect the Church against external attacks and to direct its energies toward the preservation of order and righteousness in civil life, and that the Church had the task of the instruction and cure of souls, was held by both sides. Gregorian and anti-Gregorian agreed together in the matter of the twofold rulership of the world: through priestly and through royal authority as ordained of God.

"Yet fundamentally the two parties still disagreed on the relationship of Church and State. They might well be in accord on certain matters of detail and in concrete verdicts on given situations; but even these had a different content and retrospective verdict, no matter that the terms were the same, on the part of each several party. Common concord was shared by both groups on the conception of the Church. It was on the value of the State that they differed profoundly. . . . While Gregorians proceeded to the investigation of the relation between the two as it were coerced by the realistic facts of the existence of the State as a power to be reckoned with, between which and the Church some *modus vivendi* had to be brought about, the opponents of Gregory were more than content (since it was obviously easier) to voice the claims of the State's independence on the basis of Gregory's own doctrine of the hierarchic conception of the Church. For the latter, circumstances proved unfavorable, since they followed their opponents' tactics in dealing with the subject from the Church's standpoint.

"The opposition between the two parties becomes articulate when it comes to the question of the relative rank between Church and State. Quite definitely the supporters of St. Gregory gave the preeminence to ecclesiastical authority—that is, sacerdotalism—whenever there were occasions either of specific instance or as a result of speculative contrast, inducing such a decision . . . in general the anti-Gregorians saw in the principle of the coordination of the two powers the attainment of their objective.

"In this exaltation of the Church over the State by the Gregorians and coordination of the two powers by the anti-Gregorians any genuine agreement between the two parties in the matter of the scope of the *regnum* and *sacerdotium* was completely excluded. When claims were made for the king's right of investiture, for his right to nominate to the papal see, to initiate a legal process against the Pope, to convoke synods or to proceed to measures for reform in domestic matters concerning the Church, either mixed circumstances, half spiritual or half secular come into question, or else it has to do with obligation which could conceivably be taken away from the lay leader [Vogt] of the Church either directly or indirectly. It was these rights which did not attach to the head of the State as such as if they were to the enhancement of his personal influence, but such rights as he enjoyed as the representative of the whole civil and political commonwealth which it was his duty to exercise. All such forms of the influence of worldly rulers within the scope of ecclesiastical confines were stigmatized by the papal party as an enslavement of the Church. Even in the last days of the struggle, Bruno of Segni could so phrase the issue between the two parties as to say that the royal party was working for the enslavement of the Church while that of the Pope was striving for its independence. In so doing he was only following Gregory VII whom it pleased to represent his own political scheme as a struggle for exactly this same freedom. . . . Gregory's conception of the papacy involved all spiritual authority; nay more, it should embrace everything on earth. The position of the king was not unlike that of the dependence in which the bishop should stand with reference to the Pope. He had to use his power solely in the service of the Church; at all times he was subject to papal oversight; it was his duty to abdicate if the head of the Church declared him incompetent.

"Alger of Lüttich once said: 'Just as the priests ought to be subject to the kings in earthly matters so

ought still more the kings be subject to the priests in
divine matters.' But where lay the boundaries between divine and earthly concerns? The policy of the
Gregorians was to extend the sphere of influence of
the Church over the whole life of the commonwealth
and also that of the anti-Gregorians conceded to the
head of the State actions which would not of necessity have to be conceived of as encroachments upon
ecclesiastical rights, though they might be so deemed:
that is, a collision of Church and State might well
come to pass theoretically in the actual contemporary
relations between the two. The hierarchic conception
of the Church on the one side with its aggressive tendency, and the ideal of the State with theocratic tasks
on the other stood opposite each other as jealous opponents. . . . The wrongness of this hierarchic conception of the Church must first be brought to light
before any regulation of the proper relations between
Church and State in the sense of an affirmative cor-
relation between the two can become possible."[26]

THE "YORK ANONYMOUS"

Not long after his consecration, Archbishop Matthew Parker of set purpose made a collection of rare
manuscripts and books which had to do with the
peculiar ethos of the Anglican communion. These
were to be used where they still are, at Corpus
Christi College Library, Cambridge. One of the most
striking of the manuscripts there collected received
the attention of Dr. Heinrich Böhmer who in the
Libelli de Lite in the *Monumenta Germaniae Historica*
as well as his indispensable *Kirche und Staat in England und in der Normandie* brought the attention of

scholars to the work of the man still known as the York Anonymous. His laborious and exhaustive results have been unique. Bishop Hall of Norwich translated one of these tractates in the year 1641[27] but, so far as I know, this is the only translation of any portion of his work that has as yet appeared.

The York Anonymous writes in the third group of his tracts with special reference to the Church and State squabble in England during the reign of Henry I. Seldom has there been a better instance than in his case of artificial selection on the part of those to whose interests it is to preserve a certain type of tradition for posterity, and exclude others. Were it not for the unique manuscript in Cambridge I doubt if anyone would ever have heard of the issues raised or of their solution, given by this intelligent and original thinker early in the twelfth century. To the end of perceiving that the whole of the medieval tradition lay not with those who followed the school of Hildebrand, it may be well here to epitomize something of the arguments of our author. The background for that time is the Gregorian legalism. May I here repeat what I quoted before from Gregory VII: "Who does not know that the kings and rulers have their rise under impulse from the chief of this world, namely the Devil, in ignorance of God, pride, robbery, treachery, murder, yes by almost any kind of crime have vaunted themselves as superiors in blind greed and indomitable presumption over their own equals—their fellowmen." Gregory VII is here saying in effect that the whole of the secular order—following St. Augustine's *De Civitate Dei*, IV, 4—has but a diabolical and in no sense a religious origin. The whole

of secular society and civil organization proceeds
from the Devil. Its only redemption comes through
its subservience to the Church. The organization and
the whole vital life of the world can only be redeemed
by being Christianized and thus becoming a handmaid of the hierarchy. The Gregorian view has had
an enormous following in the Western part of Christendom, but there have not been lacking those who
boldly bore witness against it.[28] What might be described as the sacredness of the secular, a concept congenial to Eastern Christianity, comes into explicit
statement in the West at the hands of the York Anonymous. Of necessity, closely allied with this view
of the ruler, there is an implicit assumption of the
divinely appointed sacredness of nationality—though
at this time "nation" meant no more than the community of those who used the same speech. Throughout all that he says, the principles which the York
Anonymous enunciates derive from concrete exigencies; for example, the issue of the Church of
Rouen and the much more conclusive conflict as between the crown and the papacy during the clash
between Anselm and Henry I.

"The Roman Church has been accorded a primacy
as the mother and teacher of all the Churches with its
Bishop as the head of all bishops, but this was accorded by the bishops of Rome and their successors
themselves with a retrospective look upon the might
of the Roman Empire and the position in the world
of the city of Rome itself. This primacy has no relationship with the period in which Christianity came
into existence. Neither Christ Himself, nor the narrow circle of his Apostles, nor even the seventy-two

disciples, nor the earliest martyrs, nor even the Arch-deacon Stephen and his fellows, whose teachings, examples, and prescriptions everyone must follow, if he would not be considered unbelieving, or one who repudiates even at the point of betraying what has been handed down. It is not the Church of Rome but the Church of Jerusalem which is really the mother of all the faithful. It is that Church which received from Christ both the faith and the gift of the Holy Spirit. From it there went out the proclamation of the faith to all other communities; there Christ Himself of-ficiated as priest and bishop, ordained the sacraments, gave over the power of the keys to the Apostles, and made them princes and judges of the world and founders of all the Churches,—including also the Ro-man Church. Despite the fact that Saints Peter and Paul were the chief persons of the Roman Church they did not thereby cease to be members of the Church of Jerusalem. Everything that the Roman Church boasts about in claiming it for itself, the Church of Jerusalem possesses. When it really comes down to the matter of the past and the history of Rome authorizes our information, that city appears as a city of blood, the headquarters of all error, the purple-clad mistress of devils and the stronghold of death and darkness. The Church of Jerusalem is more-over the mother of the Roman Church. It is she rather than Rome that is the queen spoken of in Psalm xlv. To her as the primitive Church was truly accorded the primacy, and even Peter as the chief of the Apostles obtained his title from the higher chieftainship of the original Church and honored and harkened to the Apostle James as master."[29]

May I here quote an interpretation by the great master in the study of the York Anonymous: "In the middle of the classic Middle Ages in the time of Gregory VII there comes before us this ancient conception that the monarch is God, in which among all national religions of either ancient or modern times the religious verdict upon the State finds its expression and by which, either in the lower or the higher levels and in even a less refined form that conception comes to the fore that the king is the lord of the State and its chief official—so that the monarchy as such seems to be inseparable from this idea. But this whole idea is here clothed completely in medieval guise. The king is God but not as in all folk religions because of his derivation from God or the Son of Deity, but as monotheism demands because he is only representative, 'God's official,' and this denomination of him was established in the Middle Ages through the sacramental character of his consecration by analogy to those dogmatic formulations of the twin authorities, Holy Scripture and tradition."[30]

On this basis then, the York Anonymous was convinced that the Gregorian claims rested on no valid foundation. He had the temerity to go even farther: many of the implications as well as much of the content of these claims he was thoroughly convinced were wrong. In a great deal that he writes there is a curious sound of sixteenth century and even modern thinking: Why should priests have to be celibates?: Are the sacraments all of the same quality?: Is not baptism of unique importance?: What is the fundamental authority for tradition in the Church? The York Anonymous even presents the modern assump-

tion that traditional doctrine of the sacraments
smacks of magic. I quote a brief section: "The divine
benediction, whose power is said to be greater than
that of nature (because by this benediction nature
itself is changed) confers upon the priest or the bishop
the authority and the power of the Holy Spirit by
which he is made competent to consummate the divine sacraments. Moreover, from such persons no
man is able to remove or to destroy such authority.
But if he is thus enabled he does so either through his
own power, then man becomes more powerful than
God, and man's word than God's, or if, on the other
hand, it is God's power then it is a power of God de-
stroying another power of God, and a word of God
more potent in destruction than the other word of
God—and hence there is in both a great contradiction, but to destroy God's power is a very great evil
indeed, for God's power itself is a great good and to
take away a power conferred by God is a great im-
possibility, for it is impossible that man's power
should prevail against God's. Wherefore it is not possible to depose a bishop or a priest for him who has
not the authority to take away what God has given
since deposition is nothing else than to take away
from others that power which God has Himself conferred to consummate the sacraments, inasmuch as
no man can by his own word encompass that which
his own word would not be competent to attribute."[31]
It would be very easy to quote from our author passage after passage which not only suggest but express
a modern if not definitely a Protestant outlook. In
many of his researches he emphatically belongs to the
scientific school—notably in the Twenty-ninth Trac-

tate. Here he goes back to documents and checks his case, showing that the Gregorian theory will not hold water at all so far as concerns the primacy of Canterbury over York, the issue very pressingly to the fore at the time.[32]

Of still greater importance is his theory of the monarch and his position in the life as well of the Church as of the State. The Fourth Tractate has to do with the consecration of bishops and kings and affirms very baldly and frankly a doctrine of the divine right of the ruler. "And Peter and the other Apostles before they began to exercise their priesthood yet were ruling over the disciples of Christ with Christ Himself and received from Him the keys of the kingdom of Heaven, which fact is evidence of the truth that these keys belong not to the priests but the kings."[33]

As in the case of even St. Gregory it was the Emperor who made him Pope and our author can go on to say: "Hence it is clear that kings have the sacrosanct right of ecclesiastical rule even over the very lords pontiffs and dominion over them so that they themselves faithfully and piously should rule Holy Church, the Immaculate Spouse of the Immaculate Bridegroom, her worthy of Him, the Divine of God Himself, the Heavenly One of the Heavenly. So it is therefore in no sense contrary to the rule of holiness if kings confer the signs of their holy rule—that is, the staff and ring of honor—to those who have the right and obligation to rule."[34]

"The Roman pontiff is called 'Apostolic' because he is believed to exercise the place and the office of the Apostles, the which if he truly exercises, then involves that he be also called an Apostle. And if he in verity be an Apostle of Christ he has been also sent by Christ (for Apostle in our language means one who has been sent officially), but if he has actually been sent by Christ he ought himself proclaim Christ's commandments, seek his glory, and himself do Christ's will, in order that he might really be his true Apostle. And if he enjoins the things which have to do solely with himself, if indeed he seeks his own glory, if he actually does his own and not Christ's will who would dare to confess him to be Christ's true Apostle? On the other hand, if he *does* command those things which are Christ's, and seek to do Christ's will then he is to be received by us as Christ's Apostle with all reverence and honor on account of the authority of Him who sent him. Otherwise, there isn't the slightest necessity imposed upon us that we receive him as His Apostle. It is the Holy Gospels which teach us together with the apostolic doctrine of our Christ's commands that he ought to enjoin as Christ's Apostle upon us those things which Christ Himself commanded in the Gospel and which the apostolic college has given its sanction to because this is Christ's will of obligation upon each several Christian to perform. But if he order something quite other and proclaim something quite different the Blessed Apostle Himself instructs us how we would deal with it: Gal. i:8-9. Nevertheless, the Roman pontiff has commanded many things which Christ Himself did not enjoin and there proclaimed many other things which no one of the Apostles ever announced. . . . Therefore all these evils derive from the fact that the Bishop of Rome has given commands and has sought sundry things; and none of these should in any wise have come to pass had all willed to obey the things which the Lord Christ demands and asks. And man's will is one thing, and God's another, but it is more important to obey God's will than man's (Acts v:29). Moreover, if it be a man who is such that he 'abideth not in love and so not in God, and so God dwell not in him'? " (1 John iv:16.)[35]

What might be described as the "Anglican ethos" penetrates nearly everything that the York Anonymous has written. In the first place, he feels himself extraordinarily free in reaffirming old phrases and previously asserted conclusions. Unconventionality of ideas appears throughout all that he has written. Fearlessness, courage, and a relentless candor of logic dominate every tractate. Again, he is extraordinarily devoted to Holy Scripture. Everything he writes bristles with quotations from the Bible, utilized not solely as proof texts of the point that he is urging. He saw all of his problems in the concrete. His arguments have to do with the actual and factual; he was daring and bold when it came to principle, but at the same time deft in his dependence upon the situation and its circumstances. To call into question for example the whole of the Gregorian program not only from the standpoint of its expediency but by an appeal to principle is a rather astonishing phenomenon in the early years of the twelfth century. Again, he could not envisage Christianity save in society nor concretely save in the society of his own day, place, and environment. The clash of contradictory opinion made him reassert certain of the principles laid down in the Church's past tradition, forgotten and overlaid

by later emphasis which made for their complete exclusion from the selected tradition. The same fate
followed his own writings. Had it not been for Parker
we might never have known that such a person as he
ever existed or fulminated with such vigor against the
greatly dominant Gregorian program for the subservience of the State as ignoble to the Church as the
one Holy institution existing among men.

More clearly than in any other passage the one
which now follows demonstrates the vast difference
in outlook between the York Anonymous and the
ideas of Hildebrand. I conclude this rapid consideration of the former with his own words, which constitute the closing section of the Fourth Tractate
"On the Consecration of Pontiffs and Kings." It is to
be found in Volume III of the *Libelli de Lite*, in
M.G.H., page 679. Of royal consecration he writes:

"Therefore no one can rightly be put before him
who has been blessed with such great benedictions,
consecrated and deified with such great sacraments,
for none other is blessed with more or greater benedictions or consecrated and deified with more and greater
sacraments. Nay more, in no respect is he like anyone
else for there is no one by this token to be compared
with him. Wherefore he cannot be called a layman
because he is the Lord's anointed because by grace
he is God, because he is the supreme ruler, because he
is the chief pastor, master, defender, and instructor
of Holy Church, because he is the Lord over his
brethren and should receive the adoration of all, since
he is the chief and supreme presiding prince. Therefore he cannot be said to be less than the pontiff for
the reason that the pontiff consecrates him, since it

often happens that the lesser consecrate the greater, the inferiors their superiors just as the cardinals consecrate the Pope and his suffragans consecrate the metropolitans by which it is obvious that they are not the authors but the agents of the consecration. For it is God who consummates the sacrament while it is they who minister as agents. To whom therefore he wills God imparts greater sacraments, and to whom he wills, lesser ones. Nor let the Lord Pope be offended in these matters which have been said about the king, since he himself is supreme pontiff by virtue of the fact that he is a king.''[36]

Shortly after the middle of the twelfth century (so illustrious was the work done by St. Benedict, then distinguished by the revival of the religious life and the royal favor so often accorded new foundations, we have another steady voice raised in defense of precisely the position expressed by the York Anonymous. I quote from the Emperor Frederick I in one of his communications of the date October 1157: "Since through due princely election our Kingdom and Empire have become ours from God alone (who in the Passion of Christ His Son subjected the whole world to be ruled by the two necessary swords) and since Peter the Apostle (1 Pet. ii:17) gave forth to the world this doctrine in the words: 'Fear God. Honor the king.' Whoever shall say that our imperial crown has received as a gift from the Lord Pope, sets himself both in opposition to the divine institution and the teaching of St. Peter and is also guilty of lying."[37]

Three years later at the Synod of Pavia, he is recorded to have said to the bishops that the imperial

authority conveyed with it the power of convoking
Church councils, especially in times of emergency,
and then illustrates it by the examples of Constantine,
Justinian, Charles the Great, and Otto. Nevertheless
he "committed his authority of attending to the
vastly important business in hand" to the bishops:
"For God has made you priests and has given you
authority even of judging concerning ourself. And
because in these matters which are of God it is not our
duty to judge you, we exhort you to have such care
that you acquit yourself in this matter as if expecting
from God alone judgment upon your actions."[38]

Nothing can be more clear than the fact that there
is expressed in later days the traditional medieval
theory of the Emperor ruling by divine right. It had
its proponents as well as its antagonists. Moreover,
the incidence of sharp controversy in mighty conflict
between the two powers—the State as summed up in
the Emperor and the Church as summed up in the
Pope—had brought constantly to light the necessity
for a clarification of the anti-Gregorian theory. Buried
away in the *Monumenta Germaniae Historica* may be
found a host of other events of the once powerful
propaganda in this direction. With two absolutistic
rulers, Pope and Emperor, composition of the issue
might be achieved; but in the long run undoubtedly
the many—represented by the vast group of laity—
would have been, had they known it, entirely be-
wildered by the conflict. The two rivals, Pope and
Emperor, could easily settle matters, but the papacy,
possessed with unique authority, touched every man's
life, for the Pope claimed to be not only St. Peter's
successor and vicar but the vicar as well of Christ on

earth;[39] hence eternal concerns would in the long run overmaster those of time for the ordinary man. Dynasties might come and go but the papacy was a continuous corporation. New configurations of the political landscape, new alliances, new wars and tumults and new realignments involved rearrangements of secular life—but the Church went on playing an undeviating rôle. In short, one might say that there is a tenuous tradition from the standpoint of those writing against the omnicompetence of the Church and papacy. At the same time there was a strong tradition rooted and grounded in the spiritual needs of mankind for a policy and principle with a long view, so powerfully entrenched that at last due to its reiterated assertions it should manage to prevail. In just so far as the control of culture was in the hands of the Church the process of artificial selection of documents that were deemed worthy to survive helped mold the thought of Christendom in the West to the end of depreciating the divine right of kings and exalting that of the more divine right of the papacy.

Notes to CHAPTER II

[1] Eichmann, *Kirche und Staat*, Paderborn, 1912, Vol. I, p. 126.

[2] Alcuin on *De Civitate Dei*:
"Delectabatur [Karolus M.] et libris sancti Augustini praecipue his, qui de civitate Dei praetitulati sunt." Cf. Eichmann, *op. cit.*, Vol. I. No. 5 a, p. 10.

[3] Figgis, John N., *The Political Aspects of St. Augustine's "City of God,"* Longmans Green, 1921, p. 117; Bibliography and Notes, pp. 118-32. Figgis, John N., *Churches in the Modern State*, Longmans Green, 1913.
"In the Middle Ages, the Church is used to distinguish the spirituality from the laity, and in nine cases out of ten it means the ecclesiastical body . . . so that, whereas in the Middle Ages, 'I am a Churchman' would mean 'I am *not* a layman,' nowadays the same phrase means 'I am not a Dissenter' " (pp. 184-5). "In the Middle Ages . . . a Churchman meant one who belonged to the Church in the narrower sense of its governing body—an ecclesiastic as the word implies; just as statesman today means not a member but an officer, actually or potential of the State. . . . When the Church came in contact, as it often did, with the State, it meant the clash of the ecclesiastical with the civil hierarchy of officials. . . . All this leads to the main thesis of this paper—that in the Middle Ages Church and State in the sense of two competing societies did not exist; you have instead the two official hierarchies, the two departments if you will: the Court, and the Curia, the King's officials and the Pope's. . . . It is a quarrel between two different sets of people." (*Political Aspects*, pp. 189-91.)

[4] In the year 802 (*M. G. H.*, S. S., I, 38) in the Annals of Laurenheim it is recorded that Charles the Great selected archbishops, bishops, abbots, together with secular lords to go in his name throughout the whole of the kingdom to do justice for churches, widows, orphans, the poor, and in fact the whole of the people. Charles the Great used his bishops as his own *missi*, as is clear from Leo III's letter to Bishop Rikulf of Mainz in the year 810 (*M. G. H.*, Ep. V, 67).

[5] Charles the Great, "the new Constantine through whom God has deigned to give all things to his Church" (as Pope Hadrian wrote to him in the year 778; cf. *M. G. H.*, Ep. III, 587), had a very keen sense of his responsibility to the Church. In the days of Pippin, Stephen II of Rome had granted such a position to the king, and in the year 775 Kathewulf had written to Charles: "Therefore remember always my Lord King that thou art God's King with fear and love; that thou art in God's place to protect and rule all his members, and to give account on the day of judgment, even through thy very self. And the bishop is in the second place for he is only in the place of Christ. . . . [The king's task is] to adorn the Spouse of Christ with ornaments beyond all others, that is, to establish the high privileges of the Churches . . . to rule the monastic and canonical life together with the bishops, and also the convents. Not through laymen which would be an evil deed . . . but to emend their lives through their spiritual pastors." (*M. G. H.*, Ep. IV, 508.)

[6] St. Augustine in his Epistle 93 to Vincentius of about the year 408, entitled *de vi inferenda haereticis*, sections 16 and 17, describes the persecution of obdurate heretics as most just, yet, in the second section noted, he with some reluctance really endorses the principle of compulsory conversion. He argues pragmatically, by implication, saying that it is not necessary to dogmatize about a principle.

[7] Alcuin. See note 29, Chapter 1.

[8] In modern Turkish the word *Rumi* means belonging to the Romans, that is, to the Greeks; and the noun *Rumluk* means Greek nationality; while *Yunanli* means *Greek* in our sense of the word.

[9] Mirbt, C., *Die Stellung Augustins in der Publizistik des Gregorianischen Kirchenstreits*, Leipzig, 1888, p. 111: "In dealing with practically all questions with which the controversial literature had to concern itself Augustine's influence is apparent. This is chiefly the case in the doctrine of the Church, in the matter of uttering the sentence of excommunication and in controversy concerning the objectivity of the sacraments." Yet, as Fr. Figgis has said, "In Hildebrand himself we find but little use of St. Augustine. One of his earlier letters shows that he was imbued with a conception of the relations of Pope and Emperor, which could preserve the unity of the ancient ideal. The most famous letter of all, points the other way." (This is the letter to Hermann of Metz. Cf. Figgis, *The Political Aspects of St. Augustine's "City of God,"* p. 88.)

[10] cf. Mirbt, C., *Quellen zur Geschichte des Papsttums und des römischen Katholizismus*, 1924, Tübingen, 4th ed., p. 155, ll. 37-41. On the significance of this treatise, cf. Poole, R. L., *Illustrations of the History of Medieval Thought*, London, 2nd ed., pp. 198 *ff.*

[11] cf. that section in *De Civitate Dei*, commonly called "The Mirror of Princes," i.e. V. 24.

[12] Unsuccessful in his choice of men, frequently deluded by plausible and specious argument his stormy pontificate ended grimly in extrusion from his see and city, instance his dying words: "I have loved justice and hated iniquity, therefore I die in exile." Mathew, A. H., *The Life and Times of Hildebrand: Pope Gregory VII*, London, 1910, pp. 240-1.

[13] cf. Hearnshaw, F. J. C., *The Social and Political Ideas of Some Great Medieval Thinkers*, London, 1923; also Poole, R. L., *op. cit.*

[14] cf. De Visser, J. Th., *Kerk en Staat*, Eerste Deel, Leiden, 1926, pp. 138-74; Buonaiuti, Ernesto, *La chiesa romana*, Milan, 1933, pp. 185 *ff.*

[15] This theory had received a clear statement in the Carolingian period in the letter from a group of bishops to Louis the Pious of the date 829. It is to be found in *M. G. H.*, Cap. II, 29 (c. 3): "That the body of this same Church be divided between two chief persons. Thus we know this division to have been effected, as between two personages, to wit, the priestly and the royal, as we have received it handed down from the Holy Fathers. On which matter Gelasius the venerable bishop of the Roman See writes as follows to the Emperor Anastasius: 'There are two authorities indeed, he says, O august Emperor, by which this world is chiefly ruled, namely the sacred authority

of the pontiffs and the royal authority. Of the two so much more weighty is the burden of the priests in that they even have to give accounting for human kings at the day of the divine judgment.' " Fulgentius in his book *On Predestination and Grace* writes as follows: "So far as concerns, he says, this matter in time, in the Church there is no more powerful person than the pontiff and in the Christian secular State no one can be found of greater eminence than the emperor."

¹⁶ Of great interest with reference to the putting forward in its most extreme form of the Gregorian tradition, is that represented by the dominant wing of the counter-reformation, in which the visible society of Christians on earth is equated with the mystical Body of Christ; the institution in time and space, with the eternal Spouse of Christ. Nowhere does this more clearly appear than in the most conspicuous and characteristic product of the counter-reformation, the *Spiritual Exercises* of St. Ignatius. In St. Ignatius' "Rules for thinking with the Church" appear such statements as: *La primera, depuesto todo juicio, debemos tener ánimo aparejado y pronto para obedescer en todo á la vera Esposa de Christo nuestro Señor, que es la nuestra santa Madre Iglesia hierárquica.* The text goes on to specify the duty of praising (*alabar*) all the institutions, customs, observances, rules, persons, philosophy, and even the very ornaments of the Church. Consonant with the age in which it was written, the Fifteenth Rule warns against speaking much of predestination, as the following warns about faith; lest good works be minimized and the motive for doing them depreciated. The Seventeenth Rule is in the same vein with regard to grace. Lastly, Rule Eighteen accepts "servile fear" (*temor servil*) as pragmatically valuable but the ideal is the attainment of "filial fear," on which note the last rule N. I am using for the above quotations Joseph Rickaby's *The Spiritual Exercises of St. Ignatius Loyola: Spanish and English, with a Continuous Commentary*, Benziger, 1923, 2nd ed., pp. xii-234; the relevant sections will be found on pp. 220 *ff.*, and Father Rickaby's *Notes* (pp. 225-31) will be found most valuable.

¹⁷ Gregorii VII Registr., II, 55a (Jaffe).

¹⁸ Mirbt, *op. cit.*, p. 157, ll. 5-7.

¹⁹ cf. note 2 above.

²⁰ At the Synod of Hohenaltheim in the year 916, c. 23: "If any layman by violating his oath sworn to the king and his liegelord and afterwards plots against his kingdom and treacherously utilizes any methods to encompass his death through his perversion, because he has by lifting his hand against the Anointed of the Lord committed sacrilege—let him be anathema unless he makes due satisfaction through penance . . . that is, by leaving the world, putting aside his arms, entering a monastery for a lifetime of penance and only receiving communion at his deathbed. If a bishop, presbyter, or deacon perpetrate the said crime let him be degraded." (*M. G. H.*, Const. I, 623.)

²¹ Mirbt, Carl, *Die Publizistik zur Zeitalter Gregors VII*, pp. 86-8.

²² *ibid.*, p. 91.

²³ cf. *ibid.*, pp. 93, 94.

²⁴ *ibid.*, pp. 235-342, 343-71.

[25] Mirbt, *op. cit.*, pp. 450 *ff.*

[26] *ibid.*, pp. 572-9.

[27] *The Honor of the Married Clergy Maintained*, 1641, in Wynter's edition, *The Works of the Rt. Rev. Joseph Hall*, Oxford, 1863, Vol. VIII, pp. 624-9.

[28] cf. the letter of Kathewulf to Charles (Eichmann, *op. cit.*, p. 8); Alcuin to Charles (796-7) *ibid.*, p. 10; Leo III writing to Charles (798): "As there has come to us by your royal sanction the most prudent and faithful legates of whom one particularly distinguished, namely, the most excellent Fardulf, a devout abbot most devoted to you, and has by word of mouth confidentially intimated to us that your royal excellency had commanded us through him to bestow the pallium on Bishop Arne and to institute him in the Province of Bavaria . . . we hereby freely accede to your command and concede him the use of the pall and have consecrated him archbishop canonically." (*M. G. H.*, Ep. V, 59.) Louis the German, writing to Hadrian II in 870 says (having given the reasons for his actions): "Therefore with the consent of the clergy and people we have canonically elected and advanced into the aforesaid metropolitan see, by reason of his holiness and devotion, Willibert as archbishop whom we commend properly to your Holiness and beg that there be bestowed upon him the archiepiscopal pallium in accordance with the sanction of past custom" (*M. G. H.*, Ep. VI, 248); Charles the Great at Frankfort in 794 practically enforced the repudiation of the Seventh Ecumenical Council (*M. G. H.*, Conc. III, 165).

[29] *M. G. H.*, Vol. III, Hanover, 1897, pp. 659-60.

[30] Böhmer, *Kirche und Staat in England und in der Normandie in XI und XII Jahrhundert*, Leipzig, 1899, p. 236.

[31] *ibid.*, p. 470: No. 17, *De Benedictionibus*.

[32] *ibid.*, pp. 478-81, *De Obediendo Romano Pontifice*.

[33] *Libelli de Lite*, Tome III, p. 672.

[34] *ibid.*, p. 676.

[35] *ibid.*, pp. 680-1.

[36] A few excerpts from the Fourth Tractate (*De Consecratione Pontificum et Regum*) may show in the most glaring fashion the contrast between the Epistles of Gregory and the Dictatus Papae and the radicalism of the York Anonymous. He quotes Romans xiii: 1-7, and then says: " 'Be ye therefore subject' he says, that is every soul: if therefore this means *every* there is no exception in favor of priests. So, as we see, the royal authority or that of princes has been ordained to rule even over the priests. It has been ordained, but by God. . . . Therefore the holy pontiffs are subject to kings and princes lest they resist the ordinance of God and achieve for themselves condemnation. . . . Wherefore also the most holy priests have been subjected to kings as to Christ and give them just obedience because in the king's person they perceive Him ruling and dominating all. . . . Therefore royal authority is Christ, just as 'The Lord is the strength of his people' (Psalm xxvii:8) because to Him it is said: 'Thine is the power, Thine is the Kingdom, O Lord.' For it is He who reigns in the great grace of their majesty in that He willed that men should be sharers of His power and His name, insofar as they both rule the people and are called Anointed (*Christi*)" (pp. 670-2).

It is a little later on in this same tractate he waxes so rhetorical and hyperbolic. The king is deified (as we have seen in the text above).

[37] Mirbt, C., *Quellen zur Geschichte des Papsttums und des römischen Katholizismus*, 4th ed., p. 169, No. 313.

[38] *ibid.*, No. 314.

[39] Innocent III's decretal *Venerabilem Fratrem* of March 1202 says: "Unde illis principibus ius et potestatem eligendi regem in imperatorem postmodum provovendum recognoscimus, ut debemus, ad quos de iure et antiqua consuetudine noscitur pertinere; praesertim cum ad eos ius et potestas huiusmodi ab apostolica sede pervenerit, quae Romanum imperium in persona magnifici Karoli a Graecis transtulit in Germanos" (in Mirbt, *Quellen*, Vol. IV, p. 175). The same note appears in the decretal of Innocent III, *Per Venerabilem* of the same year: "Cum ergo videatur ex his legitimandi auctoritas non tantum in spiritualibus sed in temporalibus etiam penes Romanam ecclesiam residere, ut super hoc filiis tuis gratiam faceremus ob tua et progenitorum tuorum merita, qui semper in devotione sedis apostolicae perstitisti humiliter ex parte tua idem archiepiscopus requirebat" (*ibid.*). Cf. Archbishop of Narbonne to the King of Arragon (1213) in Mansi *Concilia*, Venice, 1778, Vol. XXII, pp. 867-70. Cf. Luchaire, A., *Innocent III: La Papauté et L'Empire*, Paris, 1906, pp. 269*f.*

III

THE FULL DEVELOPMENT OF IMPERIALISTIC, CURIALIST, AND RADICAL THINKING

JOHN OF SALISBURY

IN John of Salisbury[1] the Justinianic tradition reaches another typical formulation in the Church of the West. In the many studies made since the superb edition of the *Policraticus* by C. C. J. Webb, certain points about his teaching can be sharply outlined against the thought of his own day as well as that of preceding generations. First of all, according to John "security of life" (*incolumitas vitae*) is far more significant as the aim of the State than that of *pax*. This "security" answers to what our very ultramodern psychologists tell us to be the most important element of human organization of life, social structure, and personal adjustment. John further defines it as consisting in "awareness of truth and the exercise of virtue." It may be well to pause here to contemplate a little more closely what John thought the State ought to do and be.

Not unlike his own contemporary St. Bernard, John reasons in a very modern fashion. For example, the State exists for the benefit of its members rather than the members of the citizenry for the benefit of the State. Again he had no illusions about peace. Pacifism was as much an ideal in the Middle Ages as in previous and subsequent Christianity. Your true realist—and I am using the word not only with its metaphysical connotations, but in the ordinary modern meaning of that attitude which candidly acknowledges existing facts as realities—cannot fail to see in a good deal of the peace propaganda a kind of dangerous tendency to obscure any attempt to confront the real issues which cause war by diverting the aim of the attention to the results. So in his candor and straightforwardness, John was much more concerned with the chief constructive aim of the State rather than with the means by which it was to be achieved. He did not believe in "peace at any price." He did believe that the positive aim of the State was to create security for its citizens, maintain and protect that security and supply the necessary ways by which creative social life could be developed. Furthermore, if "security" for its members were the aim of the State his further definition suggests—just as did that of Justinian—a specifically moral end, which was twofold. The State existed to make all of its subjects aware and sensitive both to truth and the exercise of virtuous conduct. It has then both an intellectual and a practical aim. Part of the State's function would by necessity then become educative. But education without action is not a matter that intrigued his interest, when both as a force in education and as one which inculcated, by stimulating the right for redressing the wrong, the exercise of the social virtues, it was obvious to John that a purely secular aim of the State (a description which would in no wise have satisfied him) needed supplementing by the high directive force of religion.

On the other side, he is in no sense unmindful of the purely human elements in history, as his perception of them demonstrates. The massive *Policraticus* and the large monograph *Metalogicon* sparkle and snap with human warmth and raillery. He pokes fun at hunters, and likens them to the centaurs among whom "seldom was there found a decent or serious one, rarely one gifted with self-control and never, so far as I know, a sober one."[2] Again and again we find this same note of good-natured human feeling and sympathy with the people whose weaknesses he excoriates. Somehow or other he manages to convey the impression that "humanity is both lovable and perplexed." Throughout his work distinguished for its originality of thought and of its presentation, there is apparent his awareness of the high dignity of human nature. Time and again we find ourselves in retrospect feeling apologetic whenever we have lost our temper or denounced some weakness in another person. As between the modern attitude of sheer objectivity (which might almost be formulated in the phrase: "poor fellow, he couldn't help it") and the exasperated but thoroughly human attitude expressed by such words as: "what on earth made you do *that*?" it is not hard for us to see that even in our exasperation we are paying humanity a tribute—the tribute of ascribing freewill and a high dignity to human nature. Do not misunderstand me, I pray you. I am not seeking to recommend a facile self-absolution for our outbursts of anger and temper: nevertheless it seems to me that there is a kind of compliment —left-handed at best—which one pays whose awareness of our foibles and weaknesses induces a humorous if sometimes too human an expression of indignation. In so doing we are moved by a consideration which might be formulated: What I expected of you was a great deal; what you have done is not up to my expectations.

If on this subjective sharing of human experience with all its quaint illogicalities our author is whimsical and fanciful, at once sympathetic and censorious, patient and compassionate, there is a phase of his attitude which is most definitely objective and purely scientific. He has very little use, for example, for superstition. As over against it, in his preface to the Second Book he says: "The really wise man will turn everything to his use and to the practice of virtue, whether it be what is said or what is being done."[3] Lying behind this terse statement is his conviction that it is the rational quality of man's life which is his perfectly human endowment. Superstition seemed to him irrational. No matter how deep his sympathy was with human frailties and foibles, he would still press upon his readers the obligation of that quality of objectivity whereby they should see things in such a wise as by awareness of them to increase wisdom, and consequently the practice of virtue. Sheer "speculativeness" or what may be translated also "speculative conjecture" is entirely alien to his thinking. Thus objectivity, paradoxically enough, is a kind of passion with John. "He would be less than human on whom the darts thrown by those from without him do not make a wound; he would not be nearly so much a man were he not moved by that which is without, yet for the really wise a doubt arises whether anything that is really human could be alien to him. In fact, the development of virtue is the only means by which this difficulty has been solved. Since both the pagan dramatist could say: 'There is nothing human that is alien to me' and our Heavenly Master taught men to love man as Himself. Whence it is obvious that the disciple would be unworthy of such a master if he 'rejoiced not in the Truth' (1 Cor. xiii:6) and does not burn with zeal against the enemies of public order."[4] That is, no true thinking, according to John, can be impervious to the appeal both of what concerns all men as well as the demands for recognition of facts. A nice balance between the subjective and the objective is latent in our author's thinking. That which is untrue or unjust arouses a bitter passion of cold intellectual resentment. Above all things, he is concerned with the "common lot" or the "common weal."[5] He writes: "Therefore, the common weal which concerns the well-being both of the many as well as the individual, means security of life. There is nothing more important to a man than his own life nor anything more important to that life than his security." This security depends entirely upon intelligence and awareness: "It is therefore the first obligation of the man who possesses wisdom to consider deeply what sort of thing he himself is, what is within him, what is outside him, what is below him, what is above him, what has been before him and what follows him."[6] The intelligence of the individual, as "a recognition of truth and the practice of virtue is the title to security for both the individual, the whole of mankind, and of rationality within the whole of tradition."[7] The cultivation of virtues of this quality, whether of intelligence or of aspiration, depends upon nature and also upon grace: "And this yearning has been divinely implanted by his nature in man but through nature alone without God's grace it cannot come to fruition."[8] In other words, to John, the natural and the supernatural were all of one piece. It is the same God who is the God of nature and also He who has to do with the supernatural. What has impeded the successful arise of intelligence and practice of virtue is the sinfulness of man.

As in many other authors, so in John of Salisbury there are implicit assumptions which are seldom scrutinized or definite. This is conspicuously the case with his conception of sin. Judging by what he is expounding as to the nature of the *common weal*, one would gather that when he uses the word "sin" he means to suggest a twofold derivation from man's original relationships, implicit and explicit, on the part of the individual, or, from the standpoint of society at large, the same tendency manifested in the corporate life. Sin was to him the non-recognition by the individual of his place in the scheme of things. This was a transgression as well of wisdom (that is, it is foolish and stupid and a betrayal of the rational), as also recalcitrance and rebellion on the conative side (that is, the stubbornness and wilfulness of human will driven by desire and waywardness). Nowhere, so far as I know, is this explicitly stated in John's own words. It is, however, apparent that in all his discussion he is not content to take either a legalistic or formalistic interpretation of either the terms he uses or his application of them. Consistent with his theory of the common weal is his keen perception of the obstacles which nullify its complete realization.

The *common weal* he defines in the Fifth Book as "a corporation of a sort, inspired by the benevolence of

God's own gift, constructed at the bidding of the highest equity, and governed by the rule of reason."[9] While this is a classical definition of State (for he says that it so seemed to Plutarch), man in his corporate capacity is far more by nature than merely a social animal since he directly ascribes social organization to God Himself, and man in society must needs be governed both by the highest ideals of righteousness and the relentless reach of reason. He goes on to say that religion stands to life as the soul to the body.[10] It is obvious how deeply the Pauline conception as developed for example in Romans xii:5 *ff.*, 1 Corinthians xii, and Ephesians, has influenced and saturated John's political philosophy. It might not be without significance to point out at this juncture the high place of reason in the medieval scheme of things. It might be truly said of the whole period that John represents that "Christian realism" would better describe it than the hackneyed phrase "the Age of Faith." Ultimately, as well as all along its path, the faith was felt to be the ultimately rational. Unresolved contradictions there were but their perspective and alignment assumed a new place in the general scheme of thought, since your medieval thinker was convinced that in the final analysis—even though the mind of man had not yet succeeded in achieving it—there not only could be no contradiction but everywhere there was a triumphant recognition of reason.

It may seem rather tedious when John goes on to expound his theory of the body organic. Detail by detail he works out his simile. Perhaps the modern reader might find him cavil too much, yet in the writings of our author, exactness and meticulousness in detail characterize large areas of his *Policraticus* in the working out of the figure of the body politic with regard to its likeness to the body physical. Needless to say, he accords the supreme place to the ultimately rational or the ultimately spiritual. In what he has to say about episcopal appointment and election there are indubitable advances of the fundamentally democratic theory of his organization of the hierarchy. The soul of society is made up of the clergy. The head of society is the ruling prince. Just as an ancient Church writer had expressed it, "As the soul is diffused in all parts of the body and is everywhere present,"[11] so the whole of society must have a voice in the election either of prince or of hierarch. The prince then rules by will of the people who delegate their sovereignty to their representative in his person: "The chief difference between the tyrant and a prince lies here that the latter keeps allegiance to the law and rules the people by their own will who gave him his office."[12] Perhaps the one thing most of us remember about John of Salisbury is his somewhat extraordinary teaching as to the treatment of tyrants. As so much misconception has ordinarily come from his words it may be well to see exactly what he did say. "The prince does battle for the laws and the liberty of the people; the tyrant thinks of nothing to do save to empty the laws of their meaning and to put the people into slavery. The prince is the likeness of divinity while the tyrant is the very likeness of the hostile adversary in the strength of Lucifer. . . . The likeness of the Godhead, the prince, is to be loved, venerated, and cherished; the tyrant on the other hand, the very image of depravity, often ought to be put to death. The origin of the tyrant is iniquity and from the very root of his being spawns poisonous and pestiferous evils and the tree itself cries aloud for some axe to bring it down."[13]

ST. BERNARD

During the pontificate of Pope Eugenius III the famous St. Bernard at the middle of the twelfth century wrote for him a brief but highly important treatise—*De Consideratione*—roughly, on "thinking things through." With all his exaltation of the papal office and dignity—for he called the Pope "the Prince of Bishops, the Heir of the Apostles, him who possessed the birthright of Abel, the authority of Noah, the patriarchal office of Abraham, the order of Melchisedek, the dignity of Aaron, the sovereignty of Moses, the judgeship of Samuel, the power of Peter, and the anointing of Christ,"[14] he asks the Pope "What is more servile and undignified on the part especially of the chief pontiff than to work constantly over worldly matters?" In St. Bernard it is perfectly clear that his reservation of a dignified place for the spiritual office as over against temporal concerns dictates a demand for the supremacy of the spiritual over the temporal which, in his mind, must needs be evinced in action. One of the most significant phrases he uses is "while law resounds every day through the palace it is not the Lord's law but that of Justinian."[15] Here we can trace quite clearly the influence of Gregory VII. It is because secular concerns are demeaning to the truly spiritual office of the papacy that St. Bernard tries to recall the Pope to the primary necessity of the terms of that office. Not unlike

Gregory VII he regards meddling with civil and political affairs as degrading and devastating to the truly spiritual function of the chief of the Church.

St. Bernard goes on further to assert that the papal power is pastoral and not princely. In his own character the Pope ought not exercise *dominatio*, for there is only one Lord and Master and that is Christ. His primary obligation is that of stewardship and rulership. The author of *De Gratia et Libero Arbitrio* was a master of psychology. He could write to his friend the Pope,—unsparingly denouncing the evils of the papal ménage but still retaining, as he evinced, a keen sense of psychological values. In many ways St. Bernard is more modern than most of the medievals. Evangelical in his religious spirit, deeply powerful as a popular preacher,[16] he still felt compelled to intervene in purely political matters for the sake of the Church. Deep among his fundamental reactions to the Church's life in time and space lay a disposition to believe that the purely secular temper was distinctly of a lower grade. Churchmen should not busy themselves with temporal and political affairs unless they recognized fully that this was not their true task. We can trace in this attitude of St. Bernard's the entail of the Augustinian and the Gregorian tradition. No one in the West has been able to think out the relation of Church and State without having been conditioned by this thinking, by St. Augustine first and Gregory VII second. To St. Bernard, the secular order was distinctly lower than the plane of spirituality on which the true Christian should live; nevertheless it was a necessity to come to terms with the former. And incidentally it might be mentioned that St. Bernard achieved this with amazing success.[17] Fundamentally, however, there is little difference in his attitude both of suspicion and of depreciation of the nature of the secular, by which would be comprised political, economic, and social life apart from its immediate and detailed control by the Church. To St. Bernard there are not two truly correlative levels of life both sanctioned by God. There is actually but one and it is that of the divine society, the Church.

We find by implication that St. Bernard, so good a psychologist in other respects as in this, is sure that the supernatural and eternal society existing in the world of time, space, and history, had perforce to live on two levels at once. The significant thing is that he denied any possible parity between the two. The implication that if God were, as He certainly was, the author of the Church, it was the Devil who was the author of the State. In other words, there is the Gregorian clash between the omnicompetent society of Christians as the Church and the belittled associations of men called civil and political life, namely, the State.

Perhaps better than any other excerpt from St. Bernard the following would be typical of his judgment as to the place of the Pope with reference both to the Church and the world: " 'What,' you say, 'you grant me precedence: do you prohibit sovereignty?' Most certainly. You speak as if preeminence in watchful care were not good preeminence. Is not the farm in the care of the steward, and the child, though he be master, subject to the tutor? Nevertheless the steward does not own the farm, nor is the tutor

master of his master. I would have you also take
precedence that you may provide, counsel, administer, serve. Let your precedence be profitable to others;
take precedence like a faithful and wise servant
'whom his Lord hath set over his household.' For
what purpose? That you may 'give them food in due
season': in other words, may manage, not command.''[18]

Civil society may be viewed as of God or as of the
Devil; when in either form it claims to be omnicompetent, how is it possible for man to reconcile
himself to a complete allegiance to it and so exclude
the claims of the supernatural society? Putting the
question the other way about: If the divine society
be omnicompetent and hold such a verdict with
reference to civil society as to make it entirely what
one might call un-divine, how is the Christian believer
to order himself with reference to the State? Our
modern problems in these regards, with the sheerly
secularist state, with the omnicompetent Church or
the omnicompetent or totalitarian State, are in no
sense novelties in the history of the Western tradition
of civilization. That the West lost much of the Justinianic tradition and the ideals of Charles the Great
as they transmitted Justinian's thought to the West
has been manifested since the Great War. A vital
note—namely, that of balanced jurisdiction and dis-
tribution of sovereignty—seems to have vanished
from the Western scene. America's solution, by the
entire separation of Church and State is far more a
fiction than a fact. The Scandinavian countries of the
North have preserved the integrity of a unified culture which is both homogeneous and also as effective

in the religious and ecclesiastical domain as in the secular and political. It is entirely impossible of course to turn back the clock, but it is quite possible to realize "how we got this way." For one thing, medieval thought was both realistic and idealistic at the same time. Much of its realism had even up through the Reformation a strong Augustinian tinge which also colored its idealism. Today it is the fashion for us to decry idealism if we are so-called "realists," and the posing of this alternative seems to me to be in large measure due to the great Western father—Augustine. That this alternative should be so present in modern thinking would seem to me to be an unmitigated calamity. The popular mind conceives of the idealist as one whose feet are not on the ground, living in a world separated from reality and inspired by motives and principles incapable of application to the actualities of life here and now. On the whole, the realism of political life involves and begets a kind of dumb and inarticulate surrendering in such fashion as to lay mankind open to become the prey of dictators whether in Church or in State. What is most desperately needed is a restatement of the principles of democracy in some such glowing fashion as both to preserve and inspire a program the which might by virtue of allegiance to it consolidate and repristinate its virtues in the fashion of the present-day challenges to its right to exist. For the lack of this program, as Fr. Demant has pointed out,[19] democracy is not only on trial but is being daily jeopardized.

When it comes to the matter of proposing a campaign for democracy, the highest tradition of medieval thinking that has been transmitted to us at the present across the struggles of the Reformation, has confronted us with a difficulty with which we must not fail to cope. The obstacles in the way seem to me to be two chief problems: the inefficiency of democracy as a method and principle of political and ecclesiastical life; and secondly, the psychological problem involved in a kind of loyalty to the whole when the whole makes no great appeal by way of a thought-out program of competent direction, for the guidance of the many. What catches man's allegiance is an immediate plan. Democracy, in the few places in the world in which it survives today, seems to lack such a coherent plan of campaign. The various forms of the political or ecclesiastical dictatorship have the strong merit of a concerted scheme and scope of action with definite goals to be attained, definite aims to be achieved, and concrete means by which these are to be brought about. In short, absolutism, whether in Church or State, has its prophets and evangelists, while democracy fails of such support.

From the standpoint of the totalitarian State or Church the democratic form of either is inefficient. The implicit contract in a democracy is utterly different from the explicit contract in that social whole whether secular or ecclesiastical which might be denominated absolutistic or totalitarian. For the preservation of the precious rights of the individual as over against the society of which he is a member is implicitly granted in a democracy—again I repeat, whether of Church polity or of political organization —; this is explicitly surrendered in the totalitarian form of either type of organization. How valuable is this preservation of individuality and personal freedom? Are not the gains the individual achieved in the days before the war in Germany of such importance as completely to outweigh the losses sustained? From my little study of the subject I gain the strong impression that life in pre-war Germany was probably at the most efficient pitch in almost any relationship of civilization that has been achieved in our twentieth century world, yet—what of the price? Is it worthwhile yielding the fundamental principle of democracy even to encompass the advantages of efficiency in an absolute State? Precisely the same comment and question might be addressed to the ecclesiastical organizations of the present. The searching investigations in these matters made by medieval thinkers are both informative and stimulative: any study of medieval thinking will force us to be aware and alive to considerations which are normative for our present culture and civilization. An important comment is that they hold not only for the relation between Church and State but for the internal organization of both.

Notes to CHAPTER III

¹ In the chapter devoted to him by Poole, R. L., *Illustrations of the History of Medieval Thought*, Oxford, 1884 and 1920; by the same, *The Early Correspondence of John of Salisbury*, 1924, and also in his edition of the *Historia Pontificalis* (1926) we have the very best possible introduction to his work and thought. Dr. Webb published the texts of the *Policraticus* (1909) and *Metalogicon* (1929). There is a further article in Hearnshaw, *op. cit.*, No. III, pp. 53-84, which supplies additional bibliography.

² *Policraticus* (edition Webb), Vol. I, pp. 393c-394a.

³ *ibid.*, 1, 415a.

⁴ *ibid.*, 1, 477 a-b.

⁵ *ibid.*, *salus publica*, Pol. I, 477c.

⁶ *ibid.*, Pol. I, 479 b.

⁷ *ibid.*, Pol. I, 479b.

⁸ *Metalogicon* (edition Webb, lv, c. 29.)

⁹ *Policraticus*, I, 54a.

¹⁰ *ibid.*, 540 b.

¹¹ *Epistle to Diognetus*, 6.

¹² *Policraticus*, I, 513b-c. Cf. Nicholas I to Bishop Adventius of Metz (864) in Migne, *P. L.*, 119, 888. Ep. 68: "Illud vero quod dicitis, regibus et principibus vos esse subjectos, eo quod dicat apostolus: Sive regi tamquam praecellenti' (1 Peter iii) placet. Verumtamen videte, utrum reges isti, et principes quibus vos subjectos esse dicitis, veraciter reges et principes sint. Videte si primum se bene regunt, deinde subditum populum: nam qui sibi nequam est, cui alii bonus erit? Videte si iure principantur: alioqui potius tyranni credendi sunt, quam reges habendi; quibus magis resistere, et ex adverso ascendere, quam subdi debemus. Alioquin si talibus subditi, et non praelati fuerimus nos, necesse est eorum vitiis faveamus. Ergo regi, quasi praecellenti, virtutibus scilicet, et non vitiis, subditi estote; sed sicut Apostolus ait, propter Deum et non contra Deum." (Quoted by Eichmann, *op. cit.*, Vol. I, pp. 92-3.)

¹³ *Policraticus*, 8 C., 17.

¹⁴ *De Consideratione*, Lib. II, Cap. VII.

¹⁵ *ibid.*, Lib. I, Cap. IV.

¹⁶ Grimley, Horatio, ed., *St. Bernard, Abbot of Clairvaux, Selections from his letters, meditations, sermons, hymns and other writings, rendered into English.* Cambridge, 1910: No. 16, pp. 39-41; No. 6, pp. 13-15; No. 29, tract on Will, Reason, and Memory, pp. 87-9; No. 35, pp. 116-18; No. 43, pp. 142-3. Cf. also *St. Bernard*, ed. Barton Mills, M.A., London, 1929, Chapter III, pp. 16-19, Chapter XVII, p. 80.

¹⁷ In the year 1130 there was a double papal election of Innocent II (1130-1143) and of Anacletus II (1130-1138), the consequences of which produced the schism resolved by the activities chiefly of St. Bernard. It would not be too much to say that by his European diplomacy Bernard won the papacy for Innocent. It was he who induced Lothair the Saxon to bring Innocent

back from his French exile to Rome, took a second journey to Italy against Roger of Sicily, won Milan for Innocent and induced the Pope to call the Lateran Council of 1139.

[18] Book III, Chapter 1, section 2, pp. 70-1.

[19] cf. Demant, Vigo Auguste, *God, Man, and Society. An Introduction to Christian Sociology*, Morehouse Publishing Co., 1934.

IV

THE DISSOLUTION OF TENSIONS AND THE ANTECEDENTS OF OUR PRESENT-DAY SITUATION

OF the great Schoolmen undoubtedly the place of preeminence is held by St. Thomas Aquinas. Despite the mordant criticisms of his younger contemporary Duns Scotus,[1] who because of his incapacity to create a rival system at all correlative to that of St. Thomas has not received due recognition, the twofold outlook of medieval constructive thinking dates actually from the thirteenth century. There were certain basic premises in St. Thomas' mind: (1) All knowledge whether through nature or by supernatural grace, derives from the same source—God. (2) Reason and revelation can therefore never be in antagonism one to the other. (3) It was quite within the compass of the human mind to ascertain all the items of knowledge fundamentally important for the satisfactory transaction of human life. Hence, he wrote his "Summa," that is, a compendium of all that man knew both for the Here as well as for the Hereafter. As has so often been said about him,[2] the Angelic Doctor was a rationalist. The movement begun by St. Anselm of Canterbury reached its full flowering in what Dr. Walsh is pleased to call "the thirteenth, the greatest of centuries."[3]

If not by lapse of time certainly by excess of vision St. Thomas has transcended his contemporaries. Nowhere is this more apparent than in the matter of

the relation of the actual existing civil order and the
will of God as manifested through reason and revelation for the guidance of mankind. If before the days
of European nationalism St. Thomas came to terms
with race and nation; if before the days of rationalism
he came to terms with not only the intellect but the
whole province of reason itself; if before the days of
the Renaissance he included within his purview all
the best of the then known antiquity—the greatness
of St. Thomas will appear in its original luster by comparison with any man in any age.

St. Thomas asks the question whether human laws
impose a necessary obedience for conscience' sake
and says: "If indeed they be just they have obliga-
tory force in the domain of conscience from the
natural law from which they are derived. . . . Laws
are said to be just both from the *end*, namely, when
they are ordered to the common good, and from their
author when the law as laid down is not outside the
authority of him who gives it. They are said to be *just*
also from the form, when they be equally propor-
tioned in imposing obedience upon those subject to
them with reference to the common good. . . . Laws
are said to be unjust in a double fashion: first, when
they are contrary to the common good, or second,
from the end, when any ruler imposes laws that are
onerous on those subject to them which do not pertain to the common good but rather have to do with
personal greed or glory."[4]

In reply to the question of the next article:
"Whether all are subject to law," he answers in the
words of St. Paul in Romans xiii and then goes on to
say that it does not seem that one may be subject to

power who is not subject to the law which the power bears. Therefore, all men ought to be subject to law.[5]

The question here is whether human laws may be properly divided into definite categories. St. Thomas' conclusion is: "Human law insofar as it is derived from the natural law is divided into the 'law of the peoples' and 'civil' law. When it has as its aim the common good it may be divided according to the differences of service, as, for example, the law with reference: to military forces, to the princes, and to the clergy; or it can be divided in accordance with the definition of jurisdiction, or of those concerning whom laws are made; or finally in accordance with the names of those who have instituted the laws." After a rather long treatment of the more or less metaphysical basis of law he goes on to say: "For those things, derived from the law of nature, have to do with 'the law of peoples' just as conclusions from principles; for example, exemptions, sales, and other such matters, without which the men cannot live with each other. This all follows from the law of nature, because man is by nature a social animal. (See Aristotle, *Politics*, Book I, Chapter ii.) Now those things which are derived from the law of nature by way of a particular determination are the province of the civil law just as each civil society demands for itself that which is most appropriate. Secondly, from human law there is derived that which has to do with the common weal of society, in accordance with which human law may be divided according to the different classes of people who especially give themselves to the common good—as for example, the priests praying for the people to God, the princes governing the people, and the soldiers fighting for their safety. This being the case, there are for each of these three classes special laws which pertain to them severally. . . . Human laws may be designated in accordance with the different governments of their civil states. Of these one type is the kingdom, when for example it is governed by one man, in accordance with which the prince's constitutions are accepted as law. Another type of rule is aristocracy, that is, the rule of the best, in accordance with which the judgments of the wise men are accepted as law and also the decrees of the senate. Another type of rule is the oligarchy, that is, the rule of a few rich and powerful persons, in accordance with which the Praetorian law becomes the rule. . . . Still another type of rule is the rule of the people which is called democracy, in accordance with which laws are actually plebiscites. Finally, there is the rule of the tyrant, which is in every way corrupt, from which no law can possibly be derived.

"But there is a certain type of rule mixed of these which is the best, namely, that in accordance with which the law is that which 'the elders have sanctioned together with the people' (Isidore, *Etymology*, Book V, Chapter x)."[6]

For St. Thomas, it is obvious that human life is essentially social and organic. To him it was unthinkable to conceive of the organization of a social framework with reference solely to the individual. Nevertheless society is not to be constructed so that it exists to be an end in itself. In the language of Hugh of St. Victor: "*Singula sint omnium et omnia singulorum.*"[7] Elsewhere he is quite clear that the best type of society is neither the oligarchy nor the rule by the aristocrats or the unrestricted democracy but that of a constitutional monarch. "When in a kingdom in which there be one conspicuous for virtue more than the others, even in this respect superior to inferior princes, and whom all those conspicuous for virtue, including the many, are able to elect and have the right of so electing, this is the best method of selecting the prince . . . and it is manifest that it should be followed in the matter of such elections."[8]

St. Thomas goes on to say: "So far as concerns the right sort of election of princes in any city or people two things should be noted. One of these is that *all* people should have some part in the rule, for by this means peace is preserved and all people love and preserve such a method of election. The second point concerns the quality of the rule or the election to the rulership—of which, as Aristotle says, there are several kinds. Of these the chief are: the kingdom, in which one man is made ruler because of his virtue: another type, the aristocracy, in which a certain few have the power of rule. Whence it is clear in accordance with virtue that the best method of selecting princes in any country or kingdom is that in which one is placed at the head and thus is ruler over all. Under him there are other princes in accordance with their virtue. But nevertheless, such rulers belong to all not only because they may be elected by all but because they actually *are* elected by all. That kind of rule is the best when it is compounded of the royal rule, so far as one is the head over all, of aristocracy insofar as all those conspicuous for virtue have their share in it, and of democracy, that is, by power of the people

insofar as the prince is to be elected by popular
suffrage and the election of the princes pertains to the
people, and this was instituted in accordance with
divine law."

Back of what St. Thomas writes stands his conviction that sovereignty inheres in the whole of the
people fundamentally. Whoever rules over the people
rules by divine authority given by God directly to
the whole of society. This diffused power of sovereignty makes itself articulate in the act of election.
The elected representatives, whether prince, aristocrats, oligarchy, democracy, senate or in whatever
other form they may be chosen, are in the final
analysis already representatives of the people to
whom has been accorded supreme power and authority.[9] Time would fail me to go on and elaborate
the Thomist doctrine on the subject. The popularly
elected ruler, or rulers, have as a chief reason for com-
mending themselves to the suffrages of the people
their conspicuous "virtue." As is in the case of other
medievals, baldly thus to translate the word is to do
St. Thomas an injustice: *virtus* means more than
"virtue" since it also means competence, power, and
ability. It is significant that in the middle of the
thirteenth century there should have been enunciated a theory so militantly of the Whig pattern; in
fact, the Angelic Doctor has been described as the
first Whig.

What he wrote and discussed in the Schools in this
quite objective fashion would seem more striking
were there attached to it any pressure of emotion or
any depth of feeling. This, I might say in passing, is
quite alive and active in St. Thomas but in two other

domains than that of sheer philosophy and theology. Restrained passion may be found in his religious poetry and his liturgical works. Its release may be found, curiously enough, in his rather amazing discussion, still objective and without excitement, on the nature of play. It would be beside the point here to discuss that, but in passing I might just say that he believed that sheer fun and emotional release through rather vigorous buffoonery was as necessary an ingredient of both individual and social life as either the exercise of the virtues (and he lists capacity for play among the virtues), or the exercise of the manual arts, intellectual work, devotion to religion, philosophy or the like.[10]

He makes a rather acute specification that in an aristocratic community the right to rule is in accordance with capacity; in an oligarchy in accordance with wealth, and in a democracy in accordance with freedom.[11] He conceived of society as an organic whole in which people were differently endowed, but the endowments given the individual were for the benefit of the whole. Scarcely ever has the principle of *noblesse oblige* been better stated. That privilege and superior endowment involve superior responsibility was to him an axiom of his whole social philosophy. It was of course to him unthinkable that any stable organization of civil society should exist apart from an explicit recognition of the primacy of God's unique rule over all things: "Since God is the effective cause of all things it is necessary that all things be subject to the divine providence, not only things of a superior level but even of human matters and those that are still lower."[12] He says that: "all things are immediately governed by God so far as concerns the character of divine rule, but so far as concerns its execution, certain things are governed through other means."[13] His preference for what might be called a limited or constitutional monarchy appears elsewhere in his writings.[14] In other words, we can see in St. Thomas the breakdown of the notion of the world dominion of a secular empire. He is not only making room for nationalism as yet unconsciously being formed in the life of Europe, but he is experiencing in advance the very principles which it was later to initiate. The most human type of state would have appeared to him to have been that of the small nation or even of a larger national group governed by a king, who was elected by the people, to whom he stood bound by limitations of either an explicit or an implicit contract. He would never have gone so far as did John of Salisbury in his recommendation of the possibility of tyrannicide. Above all, St. Thomas was an apostle of the sacredness of law and order. The strong ruler must be invested with authority from the whole, which authority he must exercise for the common weal and the common good. But so far as I know he would have contradicted the principle that the prince possessed fundamental and full sovereignty direct from God. It was the people who had given it and by them it could be taken away. It must be done by due process of law.[15]

But who is to determine whether the ruler or rulers transgress the law? Elected because of superior virtue and competence, like other human beings they may fail of the fulfilment of the promise of their possibilities.

If the use of force is disallowed, then by what power can the duly elected régime be corrected or displaced? At this point comes in the other half of St. Thomas' teaching, which is in brief that which has become normative in the Latin Church in the curialist tradition from St. Gregory VII on.[16] The Church, the supernatural society, is the normal arbiter and mentor of the civil state and all its rulers and populace. Yet St. Thomas would be the last person sharply to set off in antithesis grace and nature, law and Gospel. I might presume to go even further: he would not set off in mutual antagonism the secular and the sacred. Nevertheless, final authority as to the fundamental and ultimate aims of mankind lay in the hands of the Church for their articulate expression. Logically it would be easy to point out the thrust of contrast between his ideal secular state and that great supernatural society of the Church. But one has a feeling in reading St. Thomas that deep down underneath, he was convinced that God is nevertheless in touch with the minds of men, active even in the great pagan philosophers who were actually a part of the process of the divine providence culminating in the Incarnation. The two were inseparable. God was as much the master of Aristotle as He was of St. John, and His spirit governed the great philosopher as much as He illuminated St. Augustine.

The robust realism of St. Thomas appears all through his writings. He had no illusions and yet he never failed to portray the ideal. In one sense he was the greatest rationalist in the Christian tradition.[17] At no point is there any flight from reason. A solid training in the writings of the Angelic Doctor is possibly the best starting-point for the modern Christian thinker to launch out from, with its assurance of fixed points of reference, the solidity of logic, illuminated by the supernatural grace of faith.

May I say another few words here about the importance of reason to the medieval mind? In the bewildering confusion of present-day thinking and feeling many a political movement has succeeded by virtue of what might be described as a flight from reason. Not only the integrity of the self but the integrity of fundamental relationships seemed to St. Thomas the very essence of human life.[18] A pagan had stated that man was a social animal; Christianity had reaffirmed this in the attempted organization of medieval life on a scale at once inclusive, highly articulated and conspicuously directed toward the great purpose of God's glory and human happiness. The law, for example, of the Reformation epoch, which in many of its aspects discredited human reason and clung solely to the infallible word of God's revelation, would have seemed to St. Thomas utterly destitute. He could not have conceived that reason and revelation should be in antagonism, nor that in principle there should be fundamental opposition between Church and State. In one of the late Gilbert K. Chesterton's best detective stories, the thief, disguised as a priest, betrayed himself in a conversation with the famous Father Brown by the statement that there were things far above reason in this Universe. Rationality was basic to St. Thomas and the essential element not only of human thinking but of human behavior.

We have then in St. Thomas what is fundamentally a Christian dogma given divine sanction, namely, the principle that God has conveyed his sovereignty to the whole of the people. He believed in what might be described as a bicameralism—that is, the election by the people as a whole to supreme authority of those best fitted by virtue of their endowments effectively to exercise that delegated sovereignty for the common good.[19] Fundamentally, his theory is democratic in the best sense. If an oligarchy is ruled by the few who rule essentially for their own ends, a king turned tyrant was no less selfish. The danger of mob rule he foresaw and probably saw without disillusionment as to his fundamental principles. Realist enough to recognize the fact that some were fitter than others, by the endowments both of nature and grace in their development by active possession of given talents and capacities, he nevertheless stalwartly emphasized the fundamental principle God has assigned to the mass of humankind ultimate sovereignty and dominion.[20]

It is of course quite unnecessary to point out that in this healthy atmosphere of democratic argument there is little left of the pessimism of the Gregorian point of view. Still less is there of the pessimism of St. Augustine. He argues from St. Augustine's words in the *De Civitate Dei* that stratagems in warfare are legitimate. St. Thomas "discusses whether it be right to carry the doctrine of the Christianity of the State so far as to make vice equivalent to crime. This he decides in the negative. He was too wise to hold a puritan theory. He does this entirely on grounds derived from St. Augustine. At the same time he denies any idea of treating Augustine as an infallible guide."[21] Like the modern thinker trained in the new philosophy, St. Thomas was convinced that the ultimately rational could be the only guide of life. There is not adequate opportunity now to discuss for example his notion of "conscience" which often means both "awareness" and also "the rule of rationality." Sin likewise again and again in his writings would seem to mean the impulse to action or the act itself done *without* reference to fundamental relationships. When he talks about things "out of proportion" the Angelic Doctor touches on ground that many modern thinkers would believe to be a discovery of these days in which we live. It is perhaps then not without reason that Pschywara in his very important work called *Polarity*[22] should have derived his inspiration from the Angelic Doctor, and a constructive rethinking—with full awareness of what modern philosophers and scientists have been doing—of the fundamental principles of a Christian metaphysic.

St. Thomas Aquinas died in the year 1274 on his way to the Council of Lyons. This was convened by the Pope in order to deal with the problem of the schismatic Eastern Church, and the Greek emperor at Constantinople had pressed, for political reasons, to have some such council go into session. So we may at this juncture turn our attention to the East and review in a very summary fashion the status of Church and State in the medieval Eastern Church.

There are three main axes about which the relations between East and West revolve: the ninth century, the eleventh, and the thirteenth. In the ninth century Photius of Constantinople initiated the schism; in the eleventh, Michael Caerularius consummated it; and the thirteenth century saw its continuance even in more powerful fashion than in the first two phases, due to the unintelligent policy of the Franks during the Fourth Crusade. Eastern Christendom has never yet been able to forgive the West; the deep emotional factors involved have interposed obstacles of such vast proportion between the Churches of the East and the Latin West that the prospects of any ultimate reconciliation seem little brighter today than they were during the days of St. Thomas.

In the East a peculiar institution bearing on the relationship between Church and State grew up imperceptibly from the days of Constantine through Justinian on. Western historians are wont to call it Caesaro-Papism. This is of course a question-begging term, not at all appreciated by Eastern Christians. What it actually means is that the evolution of the Justinianic ideal has brought to pass a situation in which the preeminent authority of the emperor of Constantinople came to be nearly universal in practice, whether it were a matter of political or ecclesiastical rule. Nevertheless, it must not be forgotten that the real issue at the Seventh Ecumenical Council in 787 had to do actually with the matter of the emperor's place in the Church.[23] The legislation at that council once for all declared for the Eastern Churches that the emperor has no jurisdiction in matters of faith, dogma, or morals, when it came to the Church's teaching and tradition.[24] Despite this fact, however, in practice again and again where there has been a strong emperor and a weak patriarch, the aggressive attitude of the former has often made heavy inroads on the authority of the latter and the liberties of the

Church. When on the other hand, a weak emperor sat on the throne of the Caesars, and a strong patriarch ruled the East, the rôles were quite frequently completely reversed. Caesaro-Papism or Caesaro-Papalism really means the right of the lay voice in the affairs of the Church. Inasmuch as the State was summed up in the person of the emperor, and the laity and lower clergy constituted the State in this sense, it was only natural that the emperor of New Rome should be the spokesman for all other members of society than the upper clergy. What is represented in later Western usage in the various democratic organizations of the post-Reformation Churches, by the house of laymen, or the house of clerical and lay deputies, or by lay elders and vestries in the local Church, has as its parallel in the East this institution which allowed to the emperor so unique a position in the Church.[25] It must also be added that if the lay voice in the person of the emperor exercised tremendous influence in ecclesiastical affairs, so also did ecclesiastics exercise a great influence in all matters concerning the State, political life, and in all social and economic questions. Needless to say, this is the phenomenon now familiar to us of a unified life of both State and Church—only this is of the East while the parallel type, with the grave differences we have already noted, is represented in the West by the Gregorian scheme.

Both the Council of Lyons, for which St. Thomas had prepared a monograph,[26] and the later Council of Florence in 1439 had as their aim the reunion between Rome and Constantinople. The West accused the East in the matter of both these Reunion Councils of being animated primarily by political considerations to make overtures to the West. The East accused the West of trying to drive too sharp a bargain, and to impose conditions which would inevitably violate the whole spiritual tradition of Eastern Christendom and enforce a disavowal of their own spiritual ancestry.

The difficulties presented by any attempt to interpret Latin Christianity to the East and Eastern Christianity to the West are tremendous. Both ancient in their tradition, the parting of the ways came to pass in the very early centuries of the Church's history.[27] The ethos of Eastern Christendom and of that of the West, while essentially the same in principle, utterly diverges in any number of ways: as to the liturgy—with its God-centeredness in the East; the legalistic spirit in the West as over against what might be described as biological and canonical rather than mechanical and legalistic in the East; the inner spirit of democracy in the East as over against at least monarchy in the West; the strong nationalism of the Eastern Churches as over against the attempt to promote a supernationalism in the West. These are some of the factors making for permanent divergence and precluding mutual understanding.

To the Eastern Christian his government and his Church interpenetrate each other at every point, whether the government be monarchic, democratic, or of the form of a dictatorship. For the most part the peoples of the Eastern Christian countries are overwhelmingly Orthodox. There is a homogeneity in the population and in its inherited ideals, that is almost unknown in the West. May I hazard a possibly wild comment? To interpret the history of Russian Christianity since the suppression a little over two centuries ago of the effective governing body of the Church by the Emperor Peter the Great, one must keep in mind some of these considerations just advanced as to the relation between Church and State. Nay more—Sovietism is in one sense the Christian ideal of Church and State turned wrong side out— with Christianity deleted. The very prominence of what any observer can see of genuine religious zeal on the part of the Communists gets its entire meaning from the past tradition of the relation of Church and State in Eastern Christendom.

When Constantinople fell in 1453, the fiasco of the Reunion Council of Florence having convinced the East that nothing could be looked for from the West in the way of genuine assistance, the Russian Church in the prime of its vitality immediately took on the Roman tradition and the insignia of the double eagle of Constantinople. The Czar began to act in the spirit of the Christian Roman emperors, in the tradition of the Byzantine emperors of the Middle Ages, and made himself the defender of all Orthodox—both politically and religiously—throughout the world. When we were young and collected postage stamps it might have seemed astonishing that the double eagle of Rome appeared on the postage stamps not only of Russia but also of Austria. The Holy Roman Empire of the West claimed the same tradition of authenticity as did that of Holy Russia. The ideal of the Holy Roman Empire, the dream of a unified Church and State dedicated to God and embracing all aspects of human life, has not died even yet from among men.

Justinian's Eastern plan and Charles the Great's Western plan endure to this present. By a singular paradox both imperial schemes, with their theory of the divine right of kings, were essentially democratic. It may seem an anomaly but I believe it to be nevertheless true that in these imperial Christian attempts to create a stable order of life in accordance with the Mind of God we may discover conclusive evidence of the basic idea of Christian democracy. On the other hand, the curialist tradition in the West makes for an absolute Church, by reaction against which claims for an absolutist State had of necessity to be put forward.

Let us now return to the West. I should like to invite your attention very briefly to consider a little known phenomenon in Western civilization during the Middle Ages—the presence and survival of what the Latin Church in the West denounced as heresy. There is a formidable list that could be drawn up from the ninth century to the fourteenth of vigorous, protesting, and subversive movements of thought, principle, and organization against the dominance of the traditional medieval ideals whether in Church or State. I mention a few of the best known only: the Bogomils, the Albigenses, the Cathari, the Waldenses, the Fraticelli, the Brethren of the Common Life, the Beguins, the Brethren of the Holy Spirit. It is astounding to think that at the time when the Christian Church—falling back upon St. Augustine's dictum that it was legitimate to use force with heretics and even to persecute them—having endorsed this principle proceeded in practice to call in the strong arm of the State for the suppression of these heretical and schismatic groups.[28] H. C. Lea in his *History of the Inquisition of the Middle Ages*[29] opens up an entirely new world to the reader who comes to know for the first time the facts he presents. The interesting thing for our purposes is to note that in nearly every case of medieval heresy from Bogomils to Lollards the security not only of the Church but also of the State was threatened. A good example appears in the following quotation from Aneas Silvius given by Dr. Pius Mella.[30] He quotes Silvius as saying that the Waldenses held that "a magistrate guilty of mortal sin possesses neither secular nor ecclesiastical authority, and in consequence is not to be obeyed." The events of the sixteenth century, he goes on to say, brought the Waldensian group, however, to "profess to acknowledge the princes of the earth."

What is of significance for our purposes is that the revolting groups of the Middle Ages revolted chiefly against not only the theological theory of the Church or the political theory of the State, but against the relation which subsisted between them, whether these relations were chiefly opposed in the matter of the State or in the matter of the Church.[31] Not even in the allegedly theological revolution nor even in the risings and revolts of the heretical movements can we fail to recognize the ubiquity of the problem of Church and State.

The declaration of the sacredness and finality of the sanctions of divine authority attaching to secular sovereignty would appear then to be rather deep-rooted principles and hence necessary adjuncts to a quarrel in which they prove to be essential elements. Ultimately we are again brought back to the question of theological issues. The question first mooted by Augustine, articulated as well as answered by Gregory VII, epitomizes one way of looking at the problem of the secular state from that of the devout believer in the great Christian tradition. The answer of Dante implicitly conveys a totally different connotation, one which in fact would limit the domain of the spiritual aristocracy or the Church (conceived of primarily as the ecclesiastics) and says of it that its jurisdiction is limited. Curialist and imperialist there will always be among the sons of men. There are those of us who would like to have all things done for us and all direction of conduct taken over from us. There are others to whom the dominical precept in St. Matthew's Gospel suggests a limitation of jurisdiction and authority on the part of the supernatural corporation called the Church. In short, there were ecclesiastical fascists as well as secular fascists long before the term ever reached the knowledge of the modern mind. The fundamental likeness between the two rests, it seems to me, in this simple psychological principle: men will pay a high price to be completely taken care of either for the Here or for the Hereafter, even if that price be a surrender of their liberty and freedom.

As between the absolute State and the absolute Church which was man to choose? The absolute State would at least allegedly take care of his problems of the temporal sphere in the Here and Now. The absolute Church promised not only to do this but could go even farther and it promised his security in the Hereafter for the world to come. It is not too easy to get at the fundamental criteria by which men took sides. What caused the real conflict was the failure of either competently to discharge its obligations: when the disillusionment of the fourteenth century set in, when the claims of the imperial rule showed grave discrepancies in the matter of the actual and real, men were forced to rethink the whole problem.

During the quarrel of the papacy with Philip the Fair of France Augostino Trionfo could say of the papacy:[32] "Article 1, 'Whether the Pope is able to elect the Emperor by his own power?' " he replied: "The Emperor is the Pope's minister insofar as he is God's. As the Apostle says in the Epistle to the Romans, the thirteenth chapter, that he does not bear the sword without reason because he is the minister of God and judge in wrath against him who does evil; for God has deputed the emperor as representative of the chief pontiff. Because it is his province to restore churches that have been broken and destroyed, to build up new ones, to honor God's presence and defend them against heretics and rebels. Moreover, it is the province of the chief agent to choose his ministers and the instruments to attain his ends . . . therefore it is my opinion that the Pope whose obligation it is to order the lives of all the faithful in the present Church to the end of achieving peace has also to direct and put them to the attainment of their natural end, when there be a just and reasonable cause, on his own initiative to be able to elect the emperor . . . therefore to the first point it may be answered that the right of electing the emperor is not allowed to any and all in favor of themselves but in favor of the Church and the Christian-folk whose head is the Pope himself. Hence when it seemed well to the Pope that such action redound to the advantage of the Church and the peace of Christendom it is quite within his power to withdraw from them that right which he himself for proper cause may have conceded."

It is obvious that here we have in practice an unrestricted theocracy, absolute and unlimited. A sentence from the Bull *Unam Sanctam*, November 18, 1302, certainly allows for this setting up of a world supremacy and world monarchy on the part of the papacy; a domain complete and unlimited on the part of the Church over all affairs: "We declare, state, define, and pronounce, that for the sake of his eternal salvation it is incumbent upon every human creature to be subject to the Roman pontiff." Two years before this pronouncement—general though its terms may be in allowing the widest possible claims for the domain of the Church over each several individual in society as well as the corporate organization of the social structure—we find Arnold of Villanova writing: "And does anyone of the faithful fail to recognize that of which even the Chaldeans and the barbarians are not ignorant that the Pope is Christ on earth, not only by virtue of his peculiar position of eminence or by its symbol, but moreover is invested with the plenipotentiary jurisdiction of universal authority, since he alone among the pontiffs has been given as a light to the Gentiles and pledge to the people that there may be salvation to all even unto the end of the earth. How therefore without the risk of the greatest ruin to Catholic Christendom may any despise his authority on the part of these very souls who have been elected to the custody of the Lord's Vicar?" He goes on to say that the enemies of the supreme pontiff are actually fighting against God, and asks: "Are not they who despise the apostolic see literally forerunners of Anti-Christ?"[33]

Such extravagant claims for the papacy—which in the West meant real claims for the Church—were confronted with actualities of the situation presented by the Babylonian Exile of the papacy and by the other events of the fourteenth century. The theory and practice were not on good speaking terms. When the papacy was the docile slave of French international politics, when the obvious behavior of the curia at Avignon failed so vastly to exemplify in fact what it announced in theory, and finally in the days of the schism, some explanation and program of policy from the secularist angle must needs have come into being. On the philosophic side this was largely the work of William of Ockham, the English Franciscan. On the side of political theory Marsiglio of Padua in his *Defensor Pacis* in 1324 made the ground ready for not only an implicit but an explicit recognition of another principle as a corrective to the papal totalitarianism.[34] In Chapter III he denies that the Gospel authorizes the use of force in compelling observance of divine law. In Chapter v he affirms a limitation on the part of any minister to dispense from the precepts of this law. He had before flatly repudiated at least one broad interpretation of Boniface's Bull when he said: "The province of defining doubtful matters with reference to the divine law especially in those which are called articles of the Christian faith and other matters that need to be believed for the sake of eternal salvation belong to the general council of the faithful or else the majority or large part thereof, and there does not attach to a particular meeting thereof or to a single person of whatever status to preserve the authority of pronouncing the aforesaid definition."[35]

In Chapter VII he returns to comment that the decretals of the Romans or their pontiffs either as a whole or individually unless substantiated by a human legislator cannot be held to bind men under pain of penalty in this world. In political theory he is actually radical. The elected prince or anyone elected to any other office possesses his authority solely by the fact of his election and is not dependent upon any other confirmation or approbation for the validity of his status. Coercive jurisdiction belongs solely to the prince whether it applies to cleric or layman even if he be an heretic, and no bishop or priest as such has any right to such jurisdiction. The right of excommunication moreover or of interdict does not belong to the bishop or priest or even an assembly constituted thereof without sanction of the believing legislator. It is striking in this connection to remember that this same principle was asserted by William the Norman,[36] and reclaimed and reformulated frequently by the English sovereigns in the Middle Ages. A still further principle enunciated by William the Norman as to the invalidity as to the dissolution of feudal oaths by the power of the Church finds statement in Chapter XXXI, and finally in Chapter XLI he asserts that the Roman pontiff or any other ecclesiastic or minister in spiritual matters ought to be elevated to his position—in accordance with divine law through the faithful lawgiver or one raising him or the general council of the faithful by which also he can either be suspended or deprived in the face of some exigent transgression.[37]

In Marsiglio of Padua—condemned by Pope John XXII[38] with John of Jandon—we have a revival in the West of what might be described as the Justinianic theory. Both in William of Ockham who more than anyone else was responsible for the destruction of the solid framework of the fabric of scholastic philosophy, we have a return to the old theory of the Church as consisting of the whole body of the faithful both clerics and lay—a repristination of a non-legalistic outlook, as well as a rejuvenation of what might be called far more an Eastern than a Western conception, namely that of a unified society in which the secular was sacred. It amounts practically to an overt repudiation of the Gregorian theory. The worldly and temporal must be rescued from the imputation of illegitimacy. No less than the ecclesiastical structure that of the political and economic order, the social and temporal relationship, possesses the approval of God and have a genuine right not only to existence but to enjoy the favor of the Almighty. Gregory VII posed a question the alternative of reply to which was, whether civil society which is of the Devil or the supernatural society which was of God: which is man to choose? Marsiglio, John of Jandon, William of Ockham, the York Anonymous all said: the dilemma is artificial and there are not two alternatives. It is not a question of either and or, as if to say which hand would you wish to preserve, your right or your left; their answer was both.[39]

In the West it has always been difficult to adjust the claims of an international Church with the fact of nationalism. "Nation" in the medieval sense meant a language group, and nation in this sense actually antedated nationality. As early as St. Thomas Aquinas it was perfectly clear that the cumbersome ideal of the Holy Roman Empire of the West did not correspond to facts. Before the end of the thirteenth century St. Thomas could see, and with satisfaction, the rise of what we call nationalism.[40] The struggle both with Philip the Fair and later with Ludwig of Bavaria are good illustrations of the principle at issue: can an international Catholicism come properly to terms with the values of nationality? Of those who thought on the subject probably the most conspicuous was Dante.[41] Recognizing quite fully that the Pope had authority in matters spiritual and in denying any effort to disavow this authority of alleged divine sanction, he still went on to say that[42] "imperial authority" proceeds immediately from God. In his mind it could not be derived from that of the Pope (Chapters XIII, XV *De Monarchia*) and asserts: "The Emperor or worldly monarch owes his authority solely to the Prince of the Universe who is God." (Chapter XVI.) Remote as might seem his discussion there are still some points in it that do bear upon our present life. He writes: "If therefore man is a kind of middle ground between the corruptible and the incorruptible, inasmuch as any mean must be cognizant of the nature of its extremes, it is therefore necessary that man be cognizant of both natures and since every nature is ordered to the seeking of some final end it follows that the end of man be twofold in such wise that since he alone of all beings shares in both the incorruptible and the corruptible thus he alone of all living beings is ordered to two ends: of which the one end is that which is corruptible but the other incorruptible. . . . Inasmuch as man stands in need of a double directive principle in accordance with the double end in view he must needs have in other words the supreme pontiff who in accordance with revelation guides mankind to life eternal and the emperor who in accordance with the texts of philosophy guides the human race to the encompassment of a temporal felicity . . . and if this be so it is only God who has elected, God who confirms him who has no superior."[43] Dante went so far as to deny the alleged authority of the electors to chose the emperor, for otherwise they would have to be regarded as the shapers of the decrees of divine providence. Dante goes on to say that: "It is therefore obvious that the authority of the temporal monarch comes down to him without any intermediary from the fount of universal authority. And that fount united in the scope of its own simplicity flows out in many streams from the abundance of divine goodness."[44]

Mention has heretofore been made of the *Jus patronatus*. This institution, with the hoary antiquity of traditional precedent behind it, constituted the chief battleground certainly in the disillusionment of the fourteenth century and even before, between what the Church alleged to be the claims of the State over the Church and what the State stoutly maintained to be its rights. Back in pagan times the institution of the heathen priest in a given place to minister to a given group usually took place when the lord of the manor or the conquering intruder established for himself and his subjects some spiritual ministrations, the support of which he himself sustained. In Saxon days, for example in England, the same tradition passed over into Christian usage. Many of the older parishes were established by sundry powerful noblemen, who after their conversion carried on the same practice: a church edifice was built, a strip of land set aside for the use of the clergy, and a tithe exacted for the subsequent spiritual ministrations that were to follow for generations to come. The motive was in part to do what could be done for the benefit of the soul of the institutor, for the spiritual advantage of his own family as also for the good estate of tenants and liegemen. The endowment itself for the foundation thus established constituted an incorporeal hereditament. The right of appointment of the incumbent passed in succession to the inheritor of the original institutor, and was regarded as a legal right and perfectly proper inheritance for the following generations. It is this which is called the *jus patronatus*.[45]

Manifestly all kinds of abuses could easily ensue. An unethical lord of the manor could easily appoint to the "living" a priest after his own mind. In days of the low level of spirituality such an incumbent did not greatly trouble the important person, by any demonstration of spiritual zeal, nor did he question or criticize ideas of conduct on his part that violated the basic behavior pattern of the Christian faith. What was conveyed down through the centuries by the *jus patronatus* is in a rough way the right to elect the pastor of a given congregation by virtue of the endowment previously made for his support. Here is a typical instance of the kind of clash that can come between Church and State. The inevitable consequence in the Middle Ages was that the appointment to a living was enmeshed entirely into the feudal system, and the priest's position depended upon the will of the feudal lord. Both to gain it as well as to sustain this position it was necessary for him to submit himself to an organization of society against which such leaders, for example, as Gregory VII protested vigorously in the name of religion.[46]

The *jus patronatus* was definitely bound up with the feudal order. Nay more, even with the order of life which preceded feudalism. The articulation of the parish priesthood into a scheme of things in which the bishop or his superiors would have the right of appointment instead of the mere right of veto by showing cause, endangered the immemorial privileges of the class in society which in the person of their several progenitors had made the institution possible. In England, particularly, there were rather venomous repudiations of the Pope's claim to appoint to livings. On the papal side, what is clear is this: at the best the spiritual interests of the Church ought to be protected as over against the property interests of the wealthy group representing those who had established and founded "livings." At the worst it could degenerate into a sordid transaction whereby nonresident foreigners could be instituted into English benefices, collect all revenues and income, and be officially endowed with jurisdiction. For example, the protests of Bishop Grossteste[47] of Lincoln in the thirteenth century against papal provisions, caused him to be regarded in England as a defender of natural rights and the law of justice, while at the Court of Rome he was thought of as an exasperating and pestilential fellow who had not the slightest right to the consideration of the arguments he advanced against the papal action. Again, so far had this condition developed in the years of the Avignon exile of the papacy that in the year 1326 at Salisbury the dean, precentor, treasurer, two archdeacons and twenty-three prebendaries were papal nominees. In 1376 the French clergy were drawing from English livings a sum of $300,000 (possibly to be multiplied by 10). Absentee French cardinals held the deaneries of three of the most important cathedrals and the archdeaconries of four others. It is no wonder then that in the fourteenth century the English folk rebelled against the whole principle of what they thought the suppression of the age-long right of the *jus patronatus* on the part of the Pope and the curia.

We find in this century violent but well thought out legislation—in the Statutes of Provisors and Praemunire—aimed definitely against what was felt to be an egregious abuse. When the whole world was being used most patently by the papacy for the benefit and advantage of the French crown, it is no wonder that England rebelled.[48]

Another instance of the apparent fatality of circumstance may be found in the Black Death, the consequences of which were very serious for the Church in both respects: as in the flu epidemic during the war, it was the younger and more vigorous part of the population that was mowed down, and so the religious houses lost a high percentage of their effective personnel; but the most serious element in this situation had to do with the change in morale, which made for a further disillusionment with regard to the

Church and especially the papacy. Religion seemed to have no effect whatever in coping with the plague, in enabling people to have spiritual confidence, or in the matter of staving off the ravages of the terrible Black Death. There was a popular rise of a kind of fatalism, which one can easily detect in the literature of the latter half of the fourteenth century.[49] The customary and comfortable doctrines and practices of Latin Catholicism at this juncture seemed to fail the needs of the faithful. The combination then of the political situation in the world at large—the papacy at Avignon, the ruthless and relentless plunderings of livings in England by absentee appointments of the Pope, the constant financial demands of the curia, the high cost of religion, and the catastrophic effects of the Black Death—all generate in the fourteenth century an atmosphere in which the attitude of definite anticlericalism and articulate disillusionment made themselves manifest.

It was in this period that there flourished a man who has been called the "morning star of the Reformation." There are several phases to his thinking, but radical as he began, in the last few years of his life he held the confidence of the bulk of English folk almost to the end, and propagated outside the length what might be described as the first self-conscious nationalistic uprising against the papacy that had as yet taken its place in the scheme of history. Wycliff[50] was the author of one of the many Oxford movements. As I shall attempt, in following Professor Hearnshaw, to give a rather different interpretation of Wycliff and Lollardy than is commonly current, I shall confine

myself to a few emphases on what seem to me rather
neglected points.

There have always been in the Church those who
are primarily pastors and those who are primarily
ecclesiastics—whether intellectual or executive. It
would seem to me clear that John Wycliff belonged
to the class of the academic Churchmen. It is hard to
believe that his poor preachers were much more than
political agitators. As one reads the texts of his writings with their cold logic and dehydrated rationalism
it is a matter of wonder that he attained the influence
that he did. By way of illustrating his mind I quote
from Hearnshaw the following high points of his
analysis. He lists eight particulars, which are essential
for the understanding of Wycliff's ideals and actions:[51]
His doctrine of dominion in grace, his nationalism,
his doctrine of the State, his Erastianism, his antisacerdotalism, his individualism, his passion for
righteousness, and his conviction that the clergy
should stick solely to spiritual tasks.

As many writers have pointed out who have studied
Wycliff deeply, it is extremely difficult to get a clear
conception of what he meant by his doctrine of
"dominion in grace." In colloquial language it might
be thus expressed: all rights of rule derive from God
and therefore are subject to the withdrawal of his
authorization, if the recipient of the right to rule has
violated God's will and commandments. According to
Wycliff, there could then be no permanent authority
in the Church but practically a temporary authority
among Churchmen. Remaining in a state of grace was
the condition for the continuance of God's authorization to fulfil any ecclesiastical function or office. Of

course instances spring ready to hand (in the de-
bauched state of the Church during the Avignon
exile of the papacy) the interpretation of which would
be most plausible in the light of Wycliff's own theory.
After all he was clearly a realist. Contrary to the usual
procedure of the scholarly minded, his theories developed out of the experience of the fact, rather than
by a constructed *a priori* theory to account for the
fact as yet not experienced. In this doctrine of dominion while not original to him yet unique in the
way in which he formulated it, the significant clash
between *studium* and *sacerdotium* appears in sharp
silhouette: what in modern terms would be described
as freedom of investigation and the right to seek the
truth wherever it may be found; which in our own life
today comes into sharp conflict with the upholders of
a thesis. The clergy of necessity had to defend the
theories that the Catholic tradition was both normative and infallible. The right of free investigation
on the other hand was claimed by the universities
who did what little they could do, whithersoever it
might carry them. That this is no ancient problem
solved in the centuries past appears from what we all
know of present-day intellectual life: of the scores of
students there are those who try to prove a thesis and
there are those who try to seek the truth. It is really
the medieval conflict between *studium* and *sacerdotium*.

Typical of Wycliff's ideas as to the relation of
Church and State is the following set of scholastic
arguments in his tractate *De Officio Regis*: "For it is
obvious from faith in Holy Scripture that no one can
sin without weakening or disturbing peace with God

and in consequence with every creature. . . . Since it is impossible to keep peace with God, unless on the part of him who serves peace be had with every creature, it is clear that with sin appearing grievous harm would be done to the kingdom. This is proved first that the King does whatever his liegeman does by his authority; but the bishops, their officials, and clergy are bound in whatever cause spiritually to recognize the royal authority; therefore, the King acts through them."[52]

Wycliff was secondly a nationalist. One significant and rather curious passage strongly depreciates one phase of union with the papal Church, chiefly because the Church is essentially French as an institution and because in no sense does it really represent the nation. A national State with a national Church subordinate to it is the way in which Professor Hearnshaw describes his ideal.[53] Curiously enough he urges independence from Rome and the wisdom of looking to the East for the ideal which the English Church might follow, namely, to live "by the custom of the Greeks under its own laws." He had a doctrine of the State so complete and conclusive to his mind—starting out from the absolutism of St. Paul—that its laws were to be put ahead of the laws even of the Church. Hence the famous phrase which created such a scandal to the persecutors of the Lollards later on—the proposition that "God must obey the Devil."[54]

Closely allied with this part of his thinking is what might be called a vulgar Erastianism plus a true Erastianism. (One of the ironies in the study of Church history, if I may digress, is that all too frequently there will be found that certain heretics after whom heresies were named did not themselves believe the kind of things the heresy in question stood for. One quaint instance in point is the fact that Erastus would never have assented to what is commonly meant by Erastianism.) The most interesting document showing his view of the ruler will be found in the tractate already alluded to under the title *De Officio Regis*. He here develops a thoroughgoing omnicompetence of the State and the subordination of the hierarchy and the national Church to the great focus of the life of the whole folk, the Christian prince. Not far removed from this point of view, is very definite antisacerdotalism. I think it might be truly said that his mentality was never that of a cleric. It is strikingly like the state of mind of many a lay theologian in Eastern Christendom today where the teaching of theological subjects is a profession like the law or business, and does not necessarily relate itself to a very deep devotion to religion. Inasmuch as Wycliff had so little sympathy with the clergy—and here again, cleric though he was by ordination it was the *studium* rather than the *sacerdotium* which, as we said above, held his attention. Utilizing the technique of current philosophy and logic he could repudiate the shallow sophistries and the ultra-dogmatism of those clergy who were far more interested in proving and sustaining a case rather than attempting to get at the truth.

His individualism is striking. In putting aside the overwhelming claims to the complete control of man's life in all its aspects by the Church he fell back upon a quite different definition. It was the Augustinian expression *congregatio predestinatorum*. It is obvious that belief in predestination goes well with individualism. Many-sided though Wycliff was, there is coherence and a certain symmetry in the qualities which, as in certain chemical combinations of atoms, go to make up a given unit. Again, his thought is distinguished by a passion for righteousness. In this he is far more national than our many writers who wrote in England. Only at this point of these many-sided characteristics does there seem to be a trace of vigorous emotion, though it is greatly restrained and kept down. Crying social evils as well as the bitterest of experiences with ordinary clergy living on a low level of spirituality and using a debased coinage of spiritual currency elicited impatience and his denunciatory indictments at times become almost strident.

Last of all, coincident with what has been already outlined, borrowed from Professor Hearnshaw, *if* the Church be what he thought it was, and *if* the State be what he thought it was, then it is necessary that the clergy should confine themselves solely to their spiritual tasks and under no circumstances meddle with further concerns, whether political, social, or economic, outside the narrow province of his definition of "spiritual." Perhaps at this point we may find the nearest justification for the popular name whereby Wycliff has become known. In most other respects he is however a medieval Catholic, disillusioned, coldly rationalistic, anticipating in part the Renaissance and suggesting a deep despair of his generation with reference to the Latin Church of the West.[55]

There are several ways in which the adjustment between Church and State may be achieved. Probably the first in historical order might be described as the

practice of the principle of parity of powers. That is to
say, Church and State form one unified organized life,
and neither prince nor president nor prelate would be
in complete control of the whole at any time. It might
be also described as the principle of the interpenetra-
tion of function, for Churchman as well as statesman
had each his own right with the exercise of his authority in the domain of the other. This mutuality of
organizational activity, based definitely on principle,
in practice led to a trial of strength on frequent occasions between the two powers—of the prelate and
prince. Back in the early days before the Middle Ages
in the West a strong emperor could cow the Church.
A strong prelate might cow the emperor. At worst this
system was one of unstable equilibrium; at best it was
one of fruitful tension. The unification of the social,
economic, political, and ecclesiastical structure, so
welded together in these several aspects that its unity
was more apparent than the diversity of elements
which composed it, has been, roughly speaking, the
guiding principle of Eastern Christendom, and its
nearest parallel in the West is that of the established
Churches of a homogeneous population where the
enormously preponderant majority was not only of
one national stock but also of one professed religious
adherence.

Manifestly in this type of relationship it would be
difficult for the Church to change the State, for it is
almost impossible to discern where the Church leaves
off and the State begins, or where the State leaves off
and the Church begins. From Constantine up through
Justinian—to narrow the field—we find the confusion
almost matched by the loyalty to the government and

loyalty to the Church. If heresy be treason, treason is also heresy. One could not be a loyal "Roman" under the Constantinopolitan dynasty whether in ecclesiastical matters or in political matters without being, from the standpoint of the Church, truly loyal to the emperor and the statutes and ordinances of the empire, and from the standpoint of the State, devoutly bound by allegiance to the Church. History shows us many instances of the confusion of issues. Symbolic survivals in the West as well as in the East today can be seen in the blessing of battleflags by the bishop, in the extraordinary place occupied by the ruling prince or his representative in the worship of the Eastern Church, and the political significance of the clergy— either in the East or in the West for Church and State alike. Parity of powers conceals the fact that there are two different qualities of the authorities claimed by Church and State. The divine right of kings most clearly asserts this parity, but at best royal authority or imperial rule extends to this life and not to that of the Hereafter. Still as the Church exists in time and space as a civil institution, holding property, having the custody of wealth, inevitably coming into touch with the humdrum everyday matters—legal, social, economic, and political—the Church is of necessity enmeshed into the order definitely of the Here and Now, but at the same time it claims as its peculiar prerogative an authority concerning the Hereafter.

The perpetual danger to the Church then would be in the realm of this last term: involved as of necessity it must be in secular matters for the very reasons I have suggested, the gravest danger is that its spiritual leaders can neither criticize nor effectively guide the spiritual life of their generation. Inevitably vested interests of the ecclesiastical corporation—the protection of prerogative, of property, and of opportunity—will do much as they have done in the past to blunt the cutting edge of the incisive spiritual leadership which the supernatural corporation, the Church, should give to society at large.

On the other hand, the close and immediate contact of the Churchman with all the affairs of the State, his constant relationship to every part of its functioning will at least keep in name and never allow to fail in fact, the proclamation in the steady elements of daily life of the claims of God over the souls of men. Statesmen have used the Church many times in the past to bolster up the State. On the other hand, in this type of their relationship one can see some advantages to religion. Religion is accepted as a normal part both of education and of public life. However diluted the solution may be, still the presence of the claims of faith can never be ignored. We can see then that there are definite advantages and disadvantages both in this picture of the relation of Church and State which I have denominated as the parity of powers.

Another solution, that typically of the Middle Ages in the West, is the assertion by the Church that the only type of human organization in society is that of a theocracy. From one point of view, as has been suggested, the whole history of the Middle Ages is the history of the clash of powers between Pope and Emperor, between Church and State. As we have seen from some samples of its literature, the conflict centered on the principle of the assertion of omnicompetence by the Church, the claim to the complete control of all the affairs of man. The inferiority complex generated by the institutions and the supernatural function of the reiterated claims of the Church to a totalitarianism beyond power of modern times to duplicate, produced a violent reaction on the part of those elements in society unwilling to accept the claims of a thoroughgoing theocracy. The claims in the West between Emperor and Pope are quite different from those in the East between patriarch and prelate and imperial authority. The Eastern emperors could naturally assume what the Eastern Church readily granted: the divine right of the ruler was theologically acceptable and practically dogma. The position of the emperor in the West even where the peculiar phenomenon of the divine right of kings appeared was always uneasy of itself, always insecure, and never quite reached the point of ready acceptance by the large body of the faithful, whether ecclesiastics or laymen. As in all controversies so in this, the conflict distorted the situation. If the Pope hadn't claimed so much he would not have imputed to the Emperor so little. If the Emperor had not been accorded so little he would not have needed to have claimed so much.

Most of the statesmen of the Middle Ages in the West were ecclesiastics. Some of the opponents of the papacy and its claims were also ecclesiastics. After all, a learned person is a clerk, which is another way of saying cleric. Whichever side one might be on in the course of medieval life ecclesiastics would certainly be found with you. It stands to reason quite obviously that men who are trained as ecclesiastical statesmen make either good soldiers or politicians. Traditions of secular life are after all conveyed by seculars to seculars, and are not necessarily in the ambit of a celibate ministry. Where the Church of the West grasped to claim so much when the Renaissance and Reformation came in, she lost heavily. Man is, after all, a citizen of two worlds of which the Here and Now universe has its claims as well as that world of the Hereafter. To belittle the former in the effort to exalt the latter issued actually in the disastrous divergence of Christendom which is one of the great problems of our modern age.

Your medieval secular ruler when he could obtain a certain right of way whether by force, personality, or principle, set immediately to work to the delimitation of functioning with reference to the Church. Principles adumbrated by the anti-curialist writers of the medieval period come into clear relief in the Renaissance period, sharp application during the Reformation, and have persisted to the point of allowing to religion shorn shreds of its previous authority. Delimitation becomes limitation. Movements such as the Anglican Reformation, Gallicanism in France under Louis XIV and the various revolts in protest against the claimed omnipotence of the papacy on the part of sundry groups brought up within it, preceded by the anticlericalism of the fourteenth century, are instances to the point. The nemesis then of medieval Church claims was the counter-attack on the part of the State which has produced modern secularism.

A third type might be described as the alleged independence of Church from State. Acquaintance with our own modern American life would lead one to suspect that the separation of Church and State with us is largely specious. While religion as such cannot in conjunction with the State exercise direct impact on social and political life, the disadvantage of the situation appears in times of national emergency when churches are expected to serve the interests of the common life in a further capacity than that of primarily spiritual leadership. From the banquet in Fanueil Hall, Boston, to selected groups of New England clergy up through the Great War, from the utilization as diplomats during the Civil War up to the gentle but persistent attempts on the part of the government to elicit spoken support from the pulpits of our country, it appears that our separation of Church and State here in America is certainly more illusory than true. In the matter of public education, for example, we have in an enormously large field a duplication of what Friedrich Barbarossa attempted in the way of freedom of thought in education. It is perhaps a singular phenomenon but one to which not enough attention has been given that in the modern secular American university, attacks upon religion and its fundamental theses can be delivered and accepted by society without demur, and yet a vigorous defense—in anything like so able a fashion—of the root principle of religion immediately arouses opposition and antagonism. What would seem to one observer to be the case might be said in brief to be: modern secular education can attack religion while it allows no room for its defense. This is one of the many phases of the working out of the separation of Church and State, which on the whole allows no parity of authority, and no opportunity for the significance and importance of religion in the educational world. The State uses the Church, but the Church cannot use the State.

After all, the fundamental points of reference in the business of living, age-long of the Christian type and pattern, must have been surrendered in a social and political organization which in principle repudiates any relationship between Church and State. Modern secularist society by its own acceptance of these fundamental points of reference leaves its citizen free from the orientation of principle which his spiritual life demands. There are then inevitable conflicts. One example would be the disparity between civil divorce legislation and the marriage ideal of traditional Christendom. Another would be the traditional theological principle of the just price and the amoral modern economic and social orientation. Unrestricted competition brings about the most serious spiritual difficulties, for the principle of the sacredness of personality and of potential achievements and opportunity is entirely overlooked. Secular education largely operates on the principle of competition rather than cooperation. For the business of living, however, whether in the Here or the Hereafter, training in cooperation is vastly more important than instilling the technique of competition. This is obviously as true of social as of political and economic life. From the kindergarten on up through the university we are well trained in both competition and criticism; we often fail to attain a technique of cooperation and appreciation. Civil society, divorced from religion and its sanctions, has its modern succession of calamities for without fundamental points of reference and some generally accepted principles of spiritual guidance to which some greater authority than that solely of the temporary will of the group may be attached, involves us of the modern world not only in the calamities of a World War but in the consequences thereof in the devastation of morale as well as of property which we are at present experiencing.

A fourth theory of the relation between Church and State would be that in which the State entirely triumphs over the Church and so far as possible extinguishes it. There are gradations of these relationships from Soviet Russia down to the Concordat of June 1929 between the Vatican and Il Duce. The democracy which Christianity first preached and then demonstrated is in the greatest possible danger today. As over against it we are confronted with the secularist alternatives of a State supreme, omnicompetent, totalitarian, and either contemptuously indifferent to the Church or else actually antagonistic. The Middle Ages again give us some interpretation of our present situation today. The cult of nationality or of political and economic theory may become a religion. In the days when faith has gone cold men fall an easy prey to the flaming evangelism of a politico-economic theory which promises at least salvation in this world. To secure it one must surrender every other religious obedience. Problematic as the outcome may be there are still the elements, significantly important in the whole of man's history, of the eliciting of self-sacrifice, obedience, mass action, and personal devotion. To say that religion suffers under these conditions is a mild understatement.

How the principles of Christian democracy can be reproclaimed for the unity of the distorted and disunited Christendom constitutes one of the gravest problems before us today, we must learn from our past though we must not allow ourselves to be entirely governed by it.

Notes to CHAPTER IV

[1] Harris, Charles R., ed., *Duns Ionnes Scotus De cognitione Dei*, London, The Clarendon Press, 1927; *ibid.*, *Duns Scotus*, 2 vols., The Clarendon Press, 1927.

[2] Grabmann, Martin, *Die echten Schriften des hl. Thomas von Aquin*, Münster, 1920. Cf. Sertillanges, Antonin D., *Les grandes thèses de la philosophie thomiste*, Louis and Gay, 1928; Gilson, Etienne, *The Philosophy of St. Thomas Aquinas*, trans. by E. Bullough, Cambridge, 1924; Gilson, Etienne, *Le Thomisme: introduction au systeme de St. Thomas d'Aquin*, Strasbourg, A. Vix et Cie, 1919; Cardinal Mercier's work at Louvain, of which the most outstanding is that emanating from his pen under the title *Neo-Scholasticism*, translated and edited by the Brothers Parker, London, 1916. Cf. De Wulf, p. 149.

[3] Walsh, James Joseph, *The Thirteenth, Greatest of Centuries*, New York Catholic Summer School Press, 1907.

[4] *Summa Theologica*, 1.2.95, art. 5. Compare also for a succinct treatment of the question De Wulf, Maurice, *Medieval Philosophy Illustrated from the System of St. Thomas Aquinas*, Harvard University Press, 1922, Chapters XIII and XIV. One of the best treatments of St. Thomas' doctrine of Church and State will be found in De Visser, J., *Kerk en Staat. Eerste Deel: Buitenland*, Sijthoff's, Leiden, 1926, pp. 174-85. Most of what the author has to say is based upon *De Regimine Principum* to which he gives an excellent bibliography.

[5] *ibid.*, 1.2.Q. 96, art. 4.

[6] *ibid.*, 1.2.95, art. 4.C.

[7] Migne, *P.L.*, 195:416.

[8] *Summa Theologica*, Q. 105.1, and also *De Regimine Principum*, I. Compare also De Visser, *op. cit.*, Chapter XV.

[9] See De Wulf, *op. cit.*, Chapter XV.

[10] cf. Rickaby, J., *Aquinas Ethicus*, 2 vols., London, 1896. Here the appropriate texts of St. Thomas will be found in translation.

[11] *Summa Theologica*, 2.2.Q. 61, art. 2.

[12] *ibid.*, 1.Q. 103, art. 5; cf. also De Visser's treatment of his idea of the "common good," *op. cit.*, pp. 178-9.

[13] *ibid.*, 1.Q. 103, art. 6.

[14] As for example in *ibid.*, 2.2.Q. 50, arts. 1 and 2. Cf. Poole, R. L., *op. cit.*, pp. 243-5; the Rev. D. S. Aveling's essay Chapter IV in Hearnshaw, *op. cit.*, pp. 85-106; Dunning, *A History of Political Theories, Ancient and Medieval*, New York, 1908, pp. 189-214.

[15] *De Regimine Principum*, Lib. I.C. 6.

[16] De Visser does not seem to have caught the enormous importance of St. Thomas' awareness of nascent nationalism but he has quite clearly seen this principle. Cf. *op. cit.*, pp. 179-80.

[17] See note 2 above.

¹⁸ To St. Thomas, as to all medievals, the most important factor in reason was the place of justice in the State. In commenting on Machiavelli's work, Fr. Figgis says: "Nothing can be nobler than Machiavelli's desire for a redeemer of his people. But of justice whether in the internal government or in the external relations of a people, he took no thought. Everything is reason of state." *op. cit.*, p. 102. In this sense, "reason of state" really means a flight from reason as the medievals thought of it.

¹⁹ Since as De Wulf says: "The collectivity or sum total of individuals is too complicated, too chaotic, to exercise power itself . . . the collectivity delegates it usually, but not necessarily to a monarch. . . . 'To ordain something for the common good belongs either to the whole community, or to someone taking the place of the community.'" See De Wulf, *op. cit.*, p. 122, and *Summa*, 1.1.Q. 90, art. 3.

²⁰ *Summa Theologica*, 2.2.Q. 40, art. 3.

²¹ Figgis, J. N., *The Political Aspects of St. Augustine's "City of God,"* London, 1921, p. 95.

²² Przywara, Erich, *Analogia Entis Metaphysik*, Munich, 1932, trans. by Bouquet, A. C., *Polarity*, London, 1935.

²³ A careful reading of the sources given in Eichmann, *op. cit.*, Vol. I, would suggest that not only was this true for the East but also for the West. Cf. Capitullary of Frankfort of 794 and associated documents.

²⁴ Kidd, B. J., *The Churches of Eastern Christendom*, London, 1927. Also Alivisatos, *Canons of the Eastern Orthodox Church*. The importance of the attitude of the West was both factual and symbolic: for the West, the fact was that this particular legislation did not approve itself, as is sufficiently manifest in the words of Book II, Chapter xxi of the so-called "Karoline Books."

²⁵ On alleged Caesaro-Papalism see Leontiou, Leontios S., "Church and State in the Byzantine Empire," *The American Church Monthly*, Vol. XXVIII, July 1930, pp. 14-24.

²⁶ *De Erroribus Graecorum* (Opera Omnia Divi Thomae Aquinatis).

²⁷ Androutsos writes as follows: "What the relation is between Church and State is shown us by ecclesiastical history. What from the orthodox point of view is the proper relationship between Church and State appears clearly from the canon law of the orthodox Church. Therefore a discussion of the relations between Church and State is of necessity both historical and canonical. Still it must not fail to be noticed that the history of this relationship begins from Christianity and properly from its recognition by the State. Concerning the relations of Church and State outside of Christendom there can be no proper discussion for the simple reason that outside it there exists no Church. A self-sufficient religious fellowship organized in legal form and structure took shape only in Christendom. Religious groups outside of it are bounded by the borders of the realm or the city whose needs they serve and intermingle the things of God with the things of man and give back to Caesar the things which belong to God. On the contrary, Christianity is both world-wide and above the world. It is world-wide for it takes its rise from a given ethnic and political circle striving to embrace in it all peoples. It is also above

the world, dividing off all human relations from the Divine without admixture, prescribing their bounds in terms of their worldly aspects, presenting as the greatest aim the relationship of the soul to eternity, in one word, giving to Caesar the things that belong to Caesar and to God the things that belong to God. As an independent fellowship the Christian Church comes into diversified partnerships with that other independent association, the State, since men themselves stand in need of both these two fellowships and the two grounds in which each operates, therefore they are not sundered from each other on the basis of right, but Church and State as circumstances govern the situation in each case, determine them in either a narrower or broader fashion. Thus, there are many varieties of the relations between Church and State according to different epochs and circumstances, and the various systems are of different sorts." (Androutsos, Chrestos, *Ekklesia kai politeia ex epopseos Orthodoxou*, Athens, 1920, pp. 4-5.)

[28] cf. St. Augustine, Epistle 93 to Vincentius (about the year 408, *de vi inferenda haereticis*), sections 16 and 17; and Eichmann, *op. cit.*, I, nos. 23 and 24. Also *ibid.*, Vol. II, Nos. 3-6.

[29] Lea, H. C., *History of the Inquisition of the Middle Ages*, Harper Brothers, 1888.

[30] Mella, Pius, *The Origin, Persecutions and Doctrines of the Waldenses*, London, 1870, p. 122.

[31] Under Clement V, the Council of Vienne (1311-1312) reckoned by the Roman Catholic Church as the Fifteenth Ecumenical Council, art. 3, asserts against the Beguards and the Beguins: "That those who are in the aforesaid state of spiritual perfection and possess the spirit of liberty are not subject to the law of human obedience nor are obliged to observe the precepts of the Church; because (as they say) where the spirit of the Lord is there is liberty." This theory, condemned by the Council of Vienne, comes under the general condemnation ascribed to the condemned group under the title of *The State of Perfection*. Typical of the Middle Ages is that heresy which in claiming perfectionism for its adherents disclaimed obedience and conformity to the current laws of Church and State.

[32] Scholz, R., *Publizistik zur Zeit Philipps des Schoenen und Bonifaz VIII*, Stuttgart, 1903, pp. 172 *ff.*; *ibid.*, *Unbekannte Kirchenpolitische Streitschriften aus der Zeit Ludwigs des Bayern*, Rome, 1911, Vol. I, Chapter iv, pp. 190 *ff.*, and Vol. II (1914), pp. 481 *ff.* Cf. Questions 35 and 44, *Summa de Potestate Papae*. Cf. De Visser, *op. cit.*, pp. 188 *ff.*

[33] Mirbt, *Quellen*, 4th ed., p. 211 (no. 373).

[34] Compare for sources Scholz, *op. oit.*, Vol. II, pp. 392 48c; De Visser, *op. cit.*, pp. 190 *ff.*

[35] Marsiglio of Padua, *Defensor Pacis*, Part III, Chapters ii, iii, v, vii. The best edition in English is that of the late Dr. Ephraim Emerton, *The Defensor Pacis of Marsiglio of Padua*, Cambridge 1920.

[36] cf. Gee and Hardy's *Documents Illustrative of English Church History*, nos. xv and xvii.

[37] Compare Part III, *passim.*

[38] In the Bull of October 23, 1327, *Licet juxta doctrinam* to the Bishop of Worcester.

[39] On the controversies of the early fourteenth century the best treatises are those by Richard Scholz mentioned above.

[40] DeWulf, M., *Medieval Philosophy Illustrated from the System of T. Aquinas*, Harvard University Press, 1922, pp. 117-28.

[41] Compare E. Sharwood Smith in Hearnshaw, F. J. C., *op. cit.*, pp. 107-38.

[42] *De Monarchia*, Book III, Chapter III, ll. 22 *ff.*; Book III, Chapters XIII, XV, XVI.

[43] *ibid.*, Chapters X, XI and XVI.

[44] Possibly the best brief treatment of the facts and future implications of the early fourteenth century situation will be found in De Visser, *op. cit.*, (*Hoofdstuk IX*) *Strijdshriften over de wereldlijke heerschappij van den paus*, pp. 209-28.

[45] Compare Hunt, William, *The English Church from its Foundation to the Norman Conquest*, Macmillan, London, 1907, s.v. *Parochial System*; *The Statutes of Provisors and Praemunire* in Gee and Hardy, *Documents*, nos. xxxv, xxxix, and xl.

[46] cf. Mirbt, Carl, *Die Publitiztik in Zeitalter Gregors VII*, Leipzig, 1894.

[47] cf. Bishop Stubb's edition of Hardwick's *A History of the Christian Church—Middle Ages*, 1894, London, p. 226, note 4; p. 228, note 2; et al.

[48] cf. Gee and Hardy, *Documents*, nos. xxxii and xxxiii.

[49] cf. Manning, *The People's Faith in the Age of Wycliff*, and the Early English Text Society's publication of related sources.

[50] Wycliffe's works are enumerated in a *Catalogue* by Shirley (Oxford, 1865). The Wycliffe Text Society has published many of them in the original, among which are *De Dominio Divino*, ed. by R. L. Poole (1890), and *De Potestate Papae*, ed. by Loserth (1907). In English: *English Works Hitherto Unprinted*, ed. by F. D. Matthew, London, 1880; *Select English Works*, ed. by T. Arnold, 3 vols., 1869-1871; *Select English Writings*, ed. by Winn, London, 1929; *Tracts and Treatises of Wycliffe*, Vaughan, London, 1845; Loserth, J., *Huss and Wycliffe*, Munich, 1925; Trevelyan, *England in the Age of Wycliffe*, London, 1904.

[51] Hearnshaw, F. C. J., *op. cit.*, Chapter VIII, "John Wycliff and Divine Dominion," especially pp. 216-23.

[52] *De Officio Regis*, Wycliffe Society edition, London, 1887, Chapter VI, p. 119.

[53] Hearnshaw, *op. cit.*, p. 217.

[54] Pope Martin V, *Inter Cunctas*, February 22, 1418, art. 6.

[55] In the year 1382 in July, letters patent against the Lollards were issued by the King, at the request of the Arehbishop of Canterbury. December 1384 saw the extension of these same letters to the Province of York (cf. Gee and Hardy, *Documents*, no. xxxviii). A decade later the so-called "Lollard Conclusions" were allegedly presented to Parliament (cf. *ibid.*, no. xli). Henry IV in 1401 took action to exert what he claimed to be his own authority to punish heresy in the Act *De baeretico comburendo* (2 Henry IV, Cap. 15; *ibid.*, no. xlii, and during the discussion of this bill the Royal writ for the burning of William Sawtree was issued (*ibid.*, no. xliii).